Missionary Voices

Dedication

*To the Unreached People Groups
of a lost world*

Missionary Voices

A Popular Theology of Missions

Edited by
H. Robert Cowles
K. Neill Foster
David P. Jones

CHRISTIAN PUBLICATIONS
CAMP HILL, PENNSYLVANIA

Christian Publications
3825 Hartzdale Drive, Camp Hill, PA 17011

Faithful, biblical publishing since 1883

ISBN: 0–87509–682–4
© 1996 by Christian Publications
All rights reserved
Printed in the United States of America

96 97 98 99 00 5 4 3 2 1

Contents

The Theology of Missions

The Fourfold Gospel

Partners in Missions

Preface

Missionary Voices is an attempt to rephrase and restate the missionary task with a contemporary accent. The contributors, all passionate advocates of the missionary cause, have in effect created a fresh mosaic. We believe it is a popular theology of missions that will be helpful to thousands.

Earlier titles in this series, *Prayer Voices* and *Holiness Voices*, have had outstanding success and enjoy still enlarging circulations. Our hope is that *Missionary Voices* will be as well received.

You may not "enjoy" these messages. Some of them impact like the opening of a blast furnace. But the truth is here, clear and unvarnished. At risk is a lost world. That is reason enough to publish *Missionary Voices*.

K. Neill Foster, Publisher
May 1996

The
Theology
of
Missions

<table>
<tr><td>CHAPTER</td><td rowspan="2"># The Person
God Uses</td></tr>
<tr><td>1</td></tr>
</table>

CHAPTER 1

The Person God Uses

by A.W. Tozer

I N A WAY, I AM RESPONSIBLE FOR the title of this chapter: "The Person God Uses." But I need to make it clear that God never uses a person in the sense that a business firm uses salespeople, sending them out on their own. God always works *in* His people and *through* them. "It is God who works *in* you to will and to act according to his good purpose" (Philippians 2:13, my emphasis). Paul refers to the "mystery" of "Christ *in* you, the hope of glory." He goes on to say, "I labor, struggling with all his energy, which so powerfully works *in* me" (Colossians 1:27-29, again my emphasis).

When I speak of the person God uses, I mean the person God can work through.

Isaiah was such a man. His enlistment as one of God's "sent ones" is familiar:

> *In the year that King Uzziah died, I saw the Lord seated on a throne, high and exalted, and the train of his robe filled the temple. Above him were seraphs, each with six wings: With two wings they*

*covered their faces, with two they covered their
feet, and with two they were flying. And they were
calling to one another:*

> *"Holy, holy, holy is the LORD Almighty;
>   the whole earth is full of his glory."*

*At the sound of their voices the doorposts and
thresholds shook and the temple was filled with
smoke.*

*"Woe to me!" I cried. "I am ruined! For I am a
man of unclean lips, and I live among a people of
unclean lips, and my eyes have seen the King, the
LORD Almighty."*

*Then one of the seraphs flew to me with a live
coal in his hand, which he had taken with tongs
from the altar. With it he touched my mouth and
said, "See, this has touched your lips; your guilt is
taken away and your sin atoned for."*

*Then I heard the voice of the Lord saying,
"Whom shall I send? And who will go for us?"*

And I said, "Here am I. Send me!"

He said, "Go . . ." (Isaiah 6:1-9)

Isaiah is trying to express that which, we must acknowledge, is inexpressible. He is trying to say
what cannot be put into words. The theologians
have a word for it. They call it the *ineffable*. In
trying to express what he sees, Isaiah is limited in at
least three ways.

Wholly Other

First, what Isaiah saw was wholly other than, and
altogether different from, anything he'd ever seen

before. In our singing, praying, worshiping, preaching and thinking, we ought always to draw a sharp line between that which is God and all that which is not God. Isaiah had been familiar with that which was not God. He was familiar with some of what God had created and made. But up to this point in his life he had never been in the presence of the Uncreated One.

Isaiah discovered a violent contrast between that which is God and that which is not God, between the Uncreated and the created. Human language staggered under his effort to express what he saw and experienced.

It is impossible, as you know, to conceive of God. People may try, but they can't grasp God with their intellects. It can't be done. If I could grasp God with my intellect, I would be equal with God. I never will be, never can be equal with God. And I can never grasp God with my intellect.

And yet, Isaiah was trying to do that. He was trying hard to set forth what he saw. And the words were clumsy and inadequate. Words are always so. They're clumsy and inadequate to express what we are familiar with. How much less then can they express what is Divine!

God here was revealing Himself to Isaiah. There's a difference between God's revealing Himself to humankind and humankind discovering God. We cannot by our intellect bore through to God. Not in a million years. Not all the pooled brains of the world could do it.

Experiential Knowledge

But God, in one second of time, can reveal Himself to the human spirit. And when He does so, that man or woman knows God. But—and this distinction is important—he or she knows Him experientially, not intellectually.

So God revealed Himself. Everything written here was true and is true. But it's greater than what is written by as much as God is greater than the human mind.

Isaiah said, "I saw the Lord seated on a throne." I wish I could make Isaiah's vision at least dimly visible to all the people of the world. *God sits upon a throne.* We've let ourselves get away from God enthroned. We are afraid it's an evidence of anthropomorphism. (I never was afraid of big words. You've heard the old couplet: "Sticks and stones can break your bones, / but names can never hurt you." So let them call us what they will.)

I still believe that God sits upon a throne, invested with self-bestowed sovereignty. I believe in the sovereignty of God. I believe that God sits upon a throne determining all events. That's why I can sleep at night. If I thought world events were in the hands of world leaders, I could neither sleep nor eat. Even the best of them are not wise enough to know what to do.

God sits on His throne, and *He* determines all events. Do not the Scriptures assure us that we have been "predestined according to the plan of him who works out everything in conformity with the purpose of his will" (Ephesians 1:11)? God decides all destinies. God disposes of all cases.

Isaiah saw creatures about which I know very little. The seraphs. They are the high, exalted ones, the fire-bringers. Only here are they mentioned in the Scriptures. But I notice with considerable satisfaction that when they are seen, they are seen near God's throne. I notice they burn with rapturous love for the Godhead. They are calling to one another as they fly above the throne,

> "Holy, holy, holy is the LORD Almighty;
> the whole earth is full of his glory."

Their *hallels* shake the very foundations of the heavenly temple, and the aroma of their incense permeates every corner. I have often wondered why the dear old rabbis and the saints and hymnists of yore didn't come to a knowledge of the Trinity just from hearing the seraphs chant, "Holy, holy, holy."

I believe in the Trinity. I want you to know I'm a Trinitarian. "I believe in one God, the Father Almighty, Maker of heaven and earth, and of all things visible and invisible. And in one Lord Jesus Christ, the only begotten Son of God, begotten of His Father before all worlds, God of God, Light of Light, very God of very God, begotten, not made, being of one substance with the Father, by whom all things were made. . . . And I believe in the Holy Ghost, the Lord and Giver of life, . . . who with the Father and the Son together is worshiped and glorified. . ." (The Nicene Creed).

The older I get and the more I pray and read my Bible, the more I believe in the Trinity. Here were the seraphs, 800 years before Mary's Baby cried in the Bethlehem manger, chanting to the Trinity. Eight hundred years before the Second Person of the Trinity came to dwell among us, the seraphs were calling out the words, "Holy, holy, holy."

Ecstatic Ascription of Glory

Allow me to say a little about the word *holy*. No preacher should attempt to do such a thing, and I shall probably make a poor job of it. Here in Isaiah 6 *holy* is attributed to the Lord of Hosts. It is more than an adjective saying God is a holy God. It's more than that. It is an ecstatic ascription of glory to the triune God. And I'm not at all sure that I know what this means. But I will give you four words which, I think, may come close to the meaning.

Always remember that long after your mind has given up and quit, you can feel your way through to God with your heart. God is out yonder, infinitely transcendent above all His creatures. The old Germans used to say, "The heart is always the best theologian." You can know more with your heart than with your head. Now don't force me to explain what I mean by the heart. I don't know what I mean by the heart. But I know I have a heart and I know you have a heart. And I know David had a heart. He talked about it frequently. Even the preachers who don't believe in hearts have hearts. We all have hearts.

Moral Purity

With our heart we know that *holy* meant at the least moral purity—at least that much. It's good to know there's Someone left to think about who is absolutely pure. In our world, you have to discount everyone. The good man is a good man—but! And the good woman is a good woman—except! Even the saints had their flaws and weaknesses. Old, severe James calls Elijah "a man of like passions." It sounds a little bit as if James is trying to excuse Elijah's foibles. But it's comforting to know that Elijah, though not a perfect man, was owned by God and, in the sense I described, used of God.

Frankly, I feel more comfortable with Elijah and Jacob and Peter than I do with Joseph and Paul. No blemishes appear in Joseph's life, or Paul's after his conversion. Jacob and Elijah and Peter had their imperfections. If I find a man who is too good (and I don't find many), I feel uncomfortable around him.

There is but One who is absolutely good, absolutely holy. There is just One whose moral purity and righteousness are impeccable, faultless. God is perfection itself. And in His presence we, by comparison, have the feeling of absolute profaneness.

We could use much more repentance in our day. A Catholic prelate in South Bend, Indiana, was commenting to a Christian brother that a man who repents ought to "stay repented."

"I believe that when people repent they ought to make it stick," said the priest. "Instead of that, they come and confess and go back and do the same thing. I believe in John-the-Baptist repentance!"

I was glad to hear that. Ever since I first read my Bible, I too have believed in John-the-Baptist repentance. I'm glad some others believe in it as well.

The reason we don't have more repentance is that we repent for what we do instead of for what we are. Repentance for what we do may go deep, but repentance for what we are goes deeper. Isaiah was suddenly aware of the sharp contrast between what God was and what he was. God's absolute holiness and his own spotted, speckled impurities brought this man of God to a sense of absolute unworthiness.

A Sense of Mystery

The word *holy* also carries a sense of mystery. Mystery so inexpressible as this baffles the understanding and stuns the mind. We fall before God in speechless humility. We should always leave room for mystery in our Christian faith. When we do not we become evangelical rationalists and we can explain everything. Just ask us any question and we are quick on the trigger with an answer. I don't believe we can answer every question. There is mystery running throughout the kingdom of God just as there is mystery running throughout the kingdom of nature. The wisest scientist, if he is honest, will admit that he knows comparatively little. The Christian who with the eyes of his heart has seen God on His throne will stop being an oracle. No longer will he pretend to know everything. Neither will he condemn another who takes a position a little different from his.

We must make room for mystery, the mystery that is God. Beware when a person prays too fluently. Sometimes, of course, a sudden passion or an outpouring of the Holy Spirit brings fluency in our praying. But as a general rule, the person who prays too fluently is not seeing much.

Like Nothing We Know

Then there was also strangeness. There was something strange, like nothing we know—remote and unknown. We've tried to trim God down to our size. We've tried to get control of God and think Him down to where we can use Him as we want. We've even made Him "Somebody up there who likes us."

One woman I heard of, crawling around the New York pubs, got involved in a conversation about God. "By the way," she inquired of the man she was talking to, "do you know God?" The man allowed that he didn't think he did. "Oh, you should know God," the woman gushed. "He is just a Living Doll!"

Ever since I heard that bit of conversation, I've had a pain inside my heart. Can it be that human beings, educated Americans, people brought up in a so-called Christian society, could refer to the ineffably holy Triune God as a "Living Doll"?

My friend, there is something about God that is different. He is beyond us, He is above us, He is transcendent. We can't get through to Him on our own. We have to throw our hearts open and say, "God, shine Yourself into my understanding, for I'll never find You otherwise."

A Sense of Fearfulness

When we've seen God on the throne, we've had the fourth thing, a sense of fearfulness. There is something portentous and dreadful and terrifying here. This same Isaiah, later in his prophecy, asks the question, "Who of us can dwell with the consuming fire? / Who of us can dwell with everlasting burning?" (Isaiah 33:14). It is *not* a reference to hell. The very next verse indicates whom Isaiah is talking about:

> *He who walks righteously*
> *and speaks what is right,*
> *who rejects gain from extortion*
> *and keeps his hand from accepting bribes,*

> who stops his ears against plots of murder
> and shuts his eyes against contemplating
> evil—
> this is the man who will dwell on the heights,
> whose refuge will be the mountain fortress.
> His bread will be supplied,
> and water will not fail him.
>
> Your eyes will see the king in his beauty
> and view a land that stretches afar."
>
> (33:15-17)

God is the consuming fire, the everlasting burning! Does not Hebrews say, "Our 'God is a consuming fire'" (12:29)? And in another place, "It is a dreadful thing to fall into the hands of the living God" (10:31)?

You will remember that Ezekiel, taken into Babylonian captivity, sat by the Kebar River, despondent and dejected. Then God opened the heavens. Ezekiel saw God and he saw fire. And coming out of the fire he saw four four-faced creatures (Ezekiel 1). We Christians should be men and women out of the fire.

We should be perfectly normal, perfectly sound, perfectly safe. We should cultivate a sense of humor. We should be perfectly down-to-earth, as practical as James. On the other hand, we should have the top side of our soul open to mystery. We should have the window above open to the mystery that is God. And we should *be* a mystery. We should be a walking miracle. We never should be the kind of person who can be explained.

In my earlier life, I read extensively in the field of psychology. I became acquainted with the great psychologists—even some I couldn't understand. Psychologists are all right when they talk about your head. But when they begin to talk about Christianity, they flounder. They are trying to explain in psychological terms what is not psychological but spiritual. The Christian should have upon him an element that is beyond psychology, beyond all natural laws up into the spiritual laws.

In his book, *Natural Laws in the Spiritual World,* Henry Drummond showed how natural laws could be projected upward and seen as the laws governing the kingdom of God. He did a fairly good job of defending his thesis, and I've received some help from the book. But as we read our Bibles and pray, we will find within the kingdom of God that which is portentous. We will find that which is fearful and dreadful to a point where we cannot be flippant.

Hostile to Sin

God is holy. And because God is holy, He is actively hostile to sin. He must be. God can only burn on and burn on and burn on against sin forever. Never let any spiritual experience or any interpretation of Scripture, never let anybody lessen your hatred for sin. Even if you fall flat into it, hate it with holy hatred and get out of it fast. It was sin that brought the downfall of the race. It was sin that brought the Savior to die on a Roman cross. It is sin that has filled every jail, every hospital, every asylum for the insane. It is sin that has been behind every murder, every divorce, every crime that has been committed since the world began. In the presence of this awesome, holy God, sin can never be anything but a heinous deformity.

Well, Isaiah testifies that the seraphs, as they flew above the throne of God, called to one another,

> "Holy, holy,. holy is the LORD Almighty.
> the whole earth is full of his glory."

Isaiah was not dreaming. He was seeing something actual. There's a difference between imagining something and actually seeing something.

William Blake is a poet I happen to like.

> Tiger, tiger, burning bright,
> In the darkness of the night.

You can rattle on for a week quoting Blake. He's very good. But Blake had a screw that vibrated a little bit somewhere. I wouldn't say it was loose, but it vibrated. He believed in fairies. You could find him sitting there talking to somebody, and ask him, "Whom are you talking to, William?" And Blake would reply, "A fairy." He was talking to a fairy on his knee. But the fairy was actually in his head. There was no fairy on his knee. It's one thing to imagine something is there; it's another to be able to see what is there. Isaiah actually saw. He saw God. He saw God filling His universe.

You know, if we had our eyes open we too would see God. God is everywhere.

> The angels keep their ancient places;
> Turn but a stone, and start a wing!
> 'Tis ye, 'tis your estrangèd faces,
> That miss the many-splendored thing.
>   (Francis Thompson)

Our faces have been turned away from God. But Isaiah saw this God. He saw the God of Abraham, Isaac and Jacob, the God of his fathers. Isaiah cried out, "I am ruined!" Someone has called it "self-depreciation to the point of total devaluation."

Do you know what I fear? I fear we are going to go out and try to convert the world by techniques and methods. I'm afraid that, unconsciously, we're going to go out saying, "We can do it!"

We Cannot Do It

No! We can*not* do it! If we could go through every institution of learning and absorb all there is to learn, the knowledge would be insufficient. If we could read every book that has ever been written, we still would not have enough knowledge to enable us to do what the Holy Spirit is sending us out to do.

God is ready to use us, to use our skills and gifts. I believe that, all right. He will work through what we offer Him. But we can never do it by ourselves. First we must devalue ourselves. Those God uses have first devalued themselves. Once we get a look at the Lord, high and exalted, we learn our true value in a hurry.

Isaiah was an astonished man. He was awestruck. His whole world suddenly dissolved into a vast, eternal whiteness. And contrasted against it in vivid red and black was his sin. He said, "My eyes have seen the King, the LORD Almighty."

What kind of man was Isaiah? A thief? An idolater? A murderer? A drunkard? A liar? He was none of those things. He was a fine, young cultured fellow, a cousin to the king, a poet in his own right.

Isaiah could have been elected to any mission board. He could have been a deacon in any church. He was a good man. I wish, by nature, I were half as good as he.

But what is even the best of men over against the eternal whiteness of God? What is the purest morality over against the holiness of the unspeakably holy God? That was what was wrong with Isaiah. When he cried out, "I am ruined!" he meant that he was experiencing the devaluation of the sin-bent creature set over against the absolutely holy Creator. What we hear in those words, "I am ruined!" is the pain cry of conscious uncleanness.

New Birth Is Painful

It's a cry of pain. That's why I don't like card-signing evangelism. I believe there ought to be a cry of pain. There ought to be the pangs of childbirth. There should be the terror of seeing ourselves in violent, utter contrast to the holy, holy, holy God. Unless we have that, I don't know how deep our repentance will go. And if our repentance doesn't go deep, our Christian experience will not go deep.

Isaiah cried out in pain. Not for what he had done, for he doesn't mention a single sin. David had some sins to confess. But Isaiah doesn't name one. It was not the acts of sin that terrified Isaiah. It was what he *was*—by nature. He was a fallen human being, stained by sin. He was horribly out of place in the presence of this awesome God.

For us today, the question is not, "Do we share Isaiah's uncleanness?" It is all too evident that we do. The question for us is, "Do we have Isaiah's *awareness* of sin?"

Isaiah was unclean, and, thank God, he became aware of it. But people today are unclean and unaware of it. Uncleanness with unawareness has terrible consequences. That is what's wrong with the world. That is what's wrong with the church. We are unclean without being aware of it. Uncleanness with unawareness makes us bold and self-assured. We have a mistaken conception of our own holiness. We have a false assurance that keeps the door to hope shut. With the eyes of our hearts we need to see God on His throne. By faith and by the Spirit's inward illumination we need to behold how holy God is. After that, there will never be any question about depravity.

We're a Depraved People

I've always believed in depravity. Calvin didn't invent the idea. People think John Calvin invented depravity. But David talked about it long before Calvin was ever thought of. The first baby born into our world was born depraved. We're a depraved people. And the work of the Holy Spirit is to make us know we are depraved.

I'm speaking now of depravity among the saints. Among those who claim to be followers of Jesus. Among those who are members of His church. If only we knew the depravity that lies in the human breast!

When Isaiah cried out, "I am ruined!" God said to one of the seraphs, "Go!" And the seraph leaped down and put the burning coal on Isaiah's lips. That's poetic! If I were an artist, I would paint the seraph touching Isaiah's lips with the burning coal. I would never paint a picture of God or of Christ. But maybe of this.

Did you ever stop to think about a white-hot coal touching human lips? It's not very poetic, after all. It is painful. Imagine the scream of pain, the puff of white smoke, the smell of seared human flesh! Isaiah had to be purified the hard way. For Isaiah, it was by fire.

But Isaiah was purified. His lips, symbolic of all his nature were purified by fire. "See," said God, "this has touched your lips; your guilt is taken away and your sin atoned for." We might call it a sense of restored moral innocency. Isaiah knew he was bad, but now his sense of moral innocency is restored. Oh, the wonder of the grace of God. By His Spirit He lets us know how bad we are. He takes us through this terrifying, humiliating, devastating experience. We confess our deep iniquity. We acknowledge how bad we are. We own up not only to our committed sins but to our uncommitted sins. Then the fiery coal of God's grace touches us, and we have that sense of restored moral innocency. The forgiving love of God restores us. At last we are ready to serve the Lord.

I want you to notice that *then*—at that point— God said what He hadn't said before. There was no use in God's saying it before. But as soon as Isaiah confessed and had been cleansed from his guilt, God asks, "Who will go for us?"

And Isaiah responds, "Send me!"

There was the person God would use. He was the person whose iniquity had been taken away. Let's never take anything for granted, brother or sister. Never take anything for granted.

Do you know the one I pray for the most in my pastoral work? Do you know the one who gives me the most trouble? Do you know the one who is worst of all? You guessed right. A.W. Tozer! I'm not saying that to be humble. It is real and true. I've had more trouble with A.W. Tozer than with anyone else. I've preached all my lifetime to people who are better than I am. I preached to people who, I'm sure, never had a past equal to mine and who know God as well or better than I do.

After we arrive at this place of purity, as Isaiah did, then God says, "I will use you. You will be a channel through whom My Spirit can flow unhindered to a needy world."

May God give us a vision of Himself that will depreciate us to the point of total devaluation.

From there He can raise us up and send us out, saying, "Go!"

Missions and the Glory of God

CHAPTER

2

by Louis L. King

I N THE FIRST TEN VERSES OF JESUS' "high priestly" prayer (John 17), our Lord six times uses the words *glorify* and *glory*. He begins his prayer by saying: "Father, the time has come. Glorify your Son, that your Son may glorify you." Jesus was asking that in His sacrificial death He might be glorified in order that He, in turn, could glorify His Father God.

Jesus goes on to say to His Father, "I have brought you glory on earth by completing the work you gave me to do. And now, Father, glorify me in your presence with the glory I had with you before the world began" (17:4-5). He prays for a restoration of His preincarnate glory.

Then Jesus prays for His disciples—those, He says, "whom you gave me out of the world" (17:6). In referring to them, our Lord makes a profound statement. He says, "Glory has come to me through them" (17:10). *Jesus is glorified in His converts!* About that I will say more later.

We deduce, however, from these prayer requests of the Savior that glory is highly important to Him. His chief desire is to be glorified.

But, you ask, what is the "glory" of Christ?

To understand what Christ's "glory" is, we shall have to define the word. Then a look at several Old and New Testament examples of "glory" will sharpen the meaning of the word for us. After that, we can with greater certainty understand what Christ meant when He prayed to be glorified.

An Elusive Definition

Attempting to define the word *glory* is not the simple task we might at first think. After four decades of careful Bible study, I found I could not define *glory*. Its sense and meaning simply eluded me.

So I turned to Kittel's monumental *Theological Dictionary of the New Testament*. To my amazement I found that Kittel takes 23 pages to dissect and lay open the word. He defines *glory*, when used in reference to Deity, as

> some majestic spectacle or power that makes God's reputation highly impressive and thereby demands man's recognition.

The glory of God is evident in the heavens and on earth. Does not the inspired psalmist exclaim, "The heavens declare the glory of God; / the skies proclaim the work of his hands" (Psalm 19:1)? The vaulted heavens, magnificently garnished with orbs of dazzling light, provide a majestic spectacle and evidence of Christ's power in creation.

Our sun, 93 million miles distant from earth, is more than a hundred times larger. A jet plane, flying 600 miles an hour nonstop, could fly around the world in less than two days. To circumnavigate the sun, flying at the same speed, would require 188 days! Yet our sun is a mere speck in the starry empire of which it is a part. And beyond the galaxy our sun is in, there are myriads of other galaxies stretching into a seeming infinity of outer space too enormous for our mathematics to calculate.

The suns of our galaxy maintain such precise orbits and relationships to each other that we set our chronometers and compute our years by them. NASA technicians use them as signposts to shoot men to the moon and return them safely to earth. The heavens are a majestic spectacle and demonstration of God's power and glory.

The prophet Isaiah saw a vision of seraphs who were calling to one another:

> Holy, holy, holy is the LORD Almighty;
> the whole earth is full of his glory.
> (Isaiah 6:3)

Every dusk and every dawn, every noon and every twilight is a majestic spectacle. Every stately mountain, every sandy desert, every wide sea, every high cliff accents God's power. Every winding river and placid stream and plunging waterfall is a display of God's wisdom.

For many years northeastern United States was home to me. I loved the springtime. The flushes of budding trees—vivid green willows, white dogwood and pink laurel—were a visual symphony. Lilies and pansies added their grace notes. The songs of red-breasted robins imitated the gurgle of laughter in a baby's throat.

With every autumn, the trees that had caught and

saved up every beam of summer's light began to rehearse the sunshine of the year. They turned the countryside into a riot of dazzling red and tan and lavish yellow and purple.

Every part of this continent—indeed, every part of our world—"is full of [God's] glory." What an impressive Creator our God is!

But There Is More

The physical, material world around us reflects God's glory. God, however, did not stop there. He intervened to make Himself known to humankind. There, too, He manifested His glory.

God called a nation—Israel—out of slavery in Egypt to be His special people. Trapped at the Red Sea, with Pharaoh's forces pressing their flanks, Israel witnessed God's personal intervention.

At Mount Sinai, between Egypt and Canaan, He gave this new nation His Law. There at Sinai, God displayed His majesty and power.

The whole mountain was a gigantic torch of fire. The peak was ablaze. Thick, luminous smoke rose as from a furnace. There was thunder and there was lightning. Israel heard the sustained, crescendo blast of God's mighty trumpet. The whole mountain trembled and the rocks quaked.

From the midst of that conflagration, God gave Israel the Ten Commandments, the Law.

Paul comments that the Law, "engraved in letters on stone, came with glory" (2 Corinthians 3:7). It came with a display of power that made God's reputation highly impressive. The people of Israel had to recognize the mighty hand of God.

The Tabernacle and the Temple Were Inaugurated by God's Manifest Presence

God made Himself known to Israel all through their long desert passage. A cloud by day and a flaming fire by night offered them protection and direction. This miracle of cloud and fire that remained with the children of Israel throughout their journey made Hebrew history different in kind from that of any other nation.

When the tabernacle was dedicated, that luminous, radiant fiery cloud filled the whole of the inner shrine. "Moses could not enter the Tent of Meeting because the cloud had settled upon it, and the glory of the LORD filled the tabernacle" (Exodus 40:35).

God had given the simple symmetry of the tabernacle design to Moses on Mount Sinai. But it was not the tabernacle's architectural beauty that impressed the Israelites. Neither was it the opportunity to see Moses, the Law-giver and recognized national leader. What impressed them was the glory of the Lord God, manifest in the descended cloud resting on the tabernacle and filling its interior space.

Likewise, when Solomon's temple was dedicated, the cloud descended and filled the building:

> When Solomon finished [his dedicatory prayer], fire came down from heaven and consumed the burnt offering and the sacrifices, and the glory of the LORD filled the temple. The priests could not enter the temple of the LORD because the glory of the LORD filled it. When all the Israelites saw the fire coming down and the glory of the LORD above

the temple, they knelt on the pavement with their
faces to the ground, and they worshiped and gave
thanks to the LORD, saying,

> *"He is good;*
>   *his love endures forever."*
>
> (2 Chronicles 7:1-3)

Again, it was not the aromatic incense or the
animal sacrifices that most impressed the Israelites at
the temple's dedication. Yes, there was splendid
pomp and rich ceremony. Yes, the building was an
architectural marvel. But they were most impressed
by the majestic sight of God's glory in luminous
cloud and flaming fire. *God's presence* was the marvel.

Christ's Human Entry into Our World Was Celebrated by a Display of Glory

When Jesus Christ was born in Bethlehem, an angel
appeared to the shepherds "and the glory of the Lord
shone around them" (Luke 2:9). The darkness of that
Judean night was lit suddenly by an aurora of light.
The shepherds were enveloped by the light—and
frightened by it, too. "Terrified," Luke reports. The
angel announced to them that the long-awaited
Savior had been born. He told them where they
would find the Savior and how they would be able to
identify Him. Then the very heavens opened and the
angel of annunciation was joined by a multitude of
angels praising God and saying,

> *"Glory to God in the highest, /*
>   *and on earth peace to men on whom*
>   *his favor rests."*

So majestic a spectacle demanded—and obtained—the shepherds' immediate response. They did what ordinarily they would not have done. They left their flocks and went immediately to the nearby town to see for themselves the newborn Savior.

When Christ Inaugurated His Public Ministry, He Manifested His Glory

Jesus' public ministry began at Cana of Galilee. He and His disciples were attending a wedding banquet. And the sponsors of the banquet ran out of wine. At Jesus' command, the servants filled six large stone jars to the brim with water.

"Now draw some out and take it to the master of the banquet," Jesus directed. And the banquet master pronounced it "the best"!

John records: "This, the first of his miraculous signs, Jesus performed in Cana of Galilee. He thus revealed his glory, and his disciples put their faith in him" (John 2:11).

By turning water into wine Christ showed that He had power to create. He stood in a peculiar and special relation to nature. He was King of all nature and its processes.

John, writing under inspiration, calls this act of turning water into wine a manifestation of His glory. It was a majestic spectacle and an impressive display of His power. It secured His disciples' recognition that He was indeed the Son of God.

When Jesus Fed the 5,000, He Manifested His Glory

All four evangelists—Matthew, Mark, Luke and

John—include the feeding of the 5,000 in their Gospels. None specifically uses the word *glory* in relation to that miracle. But possibly no other of Jesus' miracles so closely coincides with Kittel's definition of *glory*: "Some majestic spectacle or power that makes God's reputation highly impressive and thereby demands man's recognition."

Mark, Luke and John state specifically that there were 5,000 men present on that occasion. Matthew agrees, but adds, "besides women and children" (6:14). Clearly well over 5,000 people were present when Jesus multiplied the five pancake-size barley loaves and the two small fish. Not only did all of the multitude eat to satisfaction, but the disciples gathered 12 basketfuls of leftovers!

Impressive? The people exclaimed, "Surely this is the Prophet who is to come into the world."

The people of Israel were aware of Moses' long-ago pronouncement: "The LORD your God will raise up for you a prophet like me from among your own brothers. You must listen to him" (Deuteronomy 18:15).

The Jews believed that the coming Prophet would provide food for the multitude. Had it not been through Moses' intercession in the desert that the starving Israelites had received manna from heaven? And there was also that Messianic psalm—Psalm 132—promising that God would place on David's throne a Descendant who would "bless [Zion] with abundant provisions; / her poor will I satisfy with food" (132:15).

When, therefore, Jesus fed so many, John records that immediately the people "intended to come and make him king by force" (John 6:15).

Jesus spectacularly multiplied five loaves of bread and two small fish to feed more than 5,000 people.

Those who benefited from this miracle saw in it the fulfillment of those two Old Testament prophecies. They recognized Jesus as the Prophet who was to come. He was indeed their Messiah-King. Jesus' miracle had made "God's reputation highly impressive," to the point of "demand[ing] man's recognition." It was a manifestation of God's glory.

We Come Now to Jesus' High Priestly Prayer

Jesus prayed, "Father, the time has come. Glorify your Son." He was praying in effect: "Father, support Me in My death by a majestic spectacle or display of power. Let my reputation be highly impressive, thereby causing people to recognize that I am Your Son."

God answered that prayer. When Christ hung on the cross there was darkness over the whole land from noon until three o'clock when He died. The temple veil, eight inches thick and so massive that 300 men were required to move it, was torn top to bottom. The earth trembled. Rocks split apart. Tombs opened up. When the centurion watching the crucifixion saw how Jesus died, he said, "Surely this man was the Son of God!" (Mark 15:39).

But in asking God to glorify His Son, Jesus was requesting something else. He was praying, "Father, by accepting My sacrifice and raising Me from the dead, enhance My reputation as the only Savior."

God answered that aspect of His prayer, too. God did raise Jesus from the dead. He sent an angel to the empty tomb to so inform those who came by. For 40 days, Jesus ate and drank and conversed with His disciples. Then He ascended into heaven in view of them all. Any lingering doubts were gone. They set out to tell the world of this Savior and Lord.

Glory Restored

Jesus went on to pray, "I have brought you glory on earth by completing the work you gave me to do. And now, Father, glorify me in your presence with the glory I had with you before the world began" (John 17:4-5).

When in the fullness of time Jesus left heaven to become our Rescuer, He laid aside His glory. The Scriptures say,

> *Being in very nature God,*
> *[he] did not consider equality with God*
> *something to be grasped,*
> *but made himself nothing,*
> *taking the very nature of a servant,*
> *being made in human likeness."*
> (Philippians 2:6-7)

Now on the eve of His sacrificial death and three days before His resurrection, He prays, in effect: "Father, pour back into me the glory I had with You in My preincarnate state. Restore to Me the majesty that had been Mine. Restore it in undiminished measure. Return to Me the infinity of heaven's power and authority that I laid aside when I came to earth in obedience to suffer and give My life a ransom for many."

We know that God answered that prayer, too. After His resurrection Jesus declared, "All authority in heaven and on earth has been given to me" (Matthew 28:18). Jesus possesses power over life and over death. He possesses power over Rome and Judea, over angels and devils and Satan. He has *all* power. It is power unrestricted, unlimited. It is power everywhere operable. The outworking of that power through the ages of church history has been so evident and abundant that if every instance were recorded, "even the whole world would not have room for the books that would be written" (John 21:25).

Jesus Is Glorified in Us

There is one other aspect of God's glory that we need to see. It is more exciting than all the others because it involves us—us who "have obeyed [God's] word" (John 17:6). Jesus says to His Father: "Glory has come to me through them" (17:10).

Jesus' meaning is obviously this: "My character and My power, deposited in those who are Mine, constitute a majestic spectacle. Men and women saved from sin and conformed to My image make My reputation highly impressive. My manifestation and the communication of Me through My disciples are My glory. I am glorified when converted sinners are conformed to My image."

The light of the sun is the glory of the sun. The color and fragrance of flowers are their beauty. So in His work in our lives the Lord Jesus Christ most manifests—and most glorifies—Himself. It is in redeeming sinners, more than in any other way, that Jesus is glorified. Redeemed sinners are the empty vessels into which He pours the fullness of His grace. His glory is displayed in those who come to Him with their sins, their sorrows, their needs, their cares. When they receive His life, His pardon and His so-great salvation, He is glorified.

It cost our Lord Jesus but a word to create the world. He said, " 'Let there be light,' and there was light" (Genesis 1:3). The Scriptures declare that "the universe was formed at God's command" (Hebrews 11:3). Although it cost our Lord but a word to create the universe, to redeem sinners cost Him His very life. Indeed, the cost was more than we can calculate, more than our finite minds can possibly conceive. It cost Jesus the immediate presence of His Father. It cost Him the worship of angels. It cost Him His throne and His rights and functions as God— prerogatives that had been His since the incalculable past. It cost Him His rightful habitation.

Things do not resist His power. Sun, moon, stars and all nature give Him no opposition. But sinners do. When Jesus puts His own eternal life into a dis-obedient, reprobate, rebellious sinner, that is a glorious display of His power. When Jesus infuses new life into a person dead in transgressions and sins, we have an impressive spectacle. When Jesus saves a person whose heart has beat out sinfulness with every stroke, we see a miracle that demands our recognition.

Saul Is a Classic Example

There is hardly a better illustration of our Lord's transforming power than Saul of Tarsus. We see him first as he participated in the martyrdom of Stephen (Acts 8:1). He did not throw any of the stones, but he kept the clothes of those who did.

Saul went from bad to worse. He "began to destroy the church" (8:3). His every breath was a murderous threat against the Lord's disciples (Acts 9:1).

One day, armed with authority from the high priest to arrest and take to Jerusalem members of the infant Christian church in Damascus, he set out for that city. But as he neared Damascus, "suddenly a light from heaven flashed around him" (Acts 9:3).

That sudden light was not the sun. The midday sun was all the time shining around him. As Alexander Whyte puts it, "It was a beam of the Everlasting Light of that land where they need no candle, neither light of the sun, for the glory of God doth lighten it and the Lamb is the Light thereof."

That Light cast Saul to the earth, and with his fall there was a sudden and total overthrow of his whole interior life. His onrushing, mad career was ended in a second. All the rest of his days he was totally different—a Christ-enamored man.

Thus it was that Jesus Christ was glorified in the apostle to the Gentiles. And thus it is that Jesus Christ is glorified every time a sinner is changed by His saving grace and power.

Jesus said, "I am glorified in them." His power and grace are glorified. His faithfulness, His goodness, His mercy are glorified. His sacrifice and His mission, His divine and inexhaustible love are glorified.

"I am glorified in them." It is not what He gets from His followers but what He bestows upon them that glorifies Him. The utmost a redeemed sinner can do to glorify Jesus is live His life and abide in Him. Jesus is glorified when we go to Him for comfort and guidance, when we look to Him for faith and hope. He is the fountain opened for sin and uncleanness. He alone is our righteousness.

We must live His life. We must walk in His light.

Every victory is His triumph. Every experience of healing is His work. It is not our fruitfulness, but His. It is not our growth, save as we grow in Him. It is not our success but His. It is His gladness, His comfort. Everything is in Christ Jesus, to whom be glory both now and forever!

The Glory of Christ: One Motive for Missions

There are many reasons for taking the good news of Jesus Christ to the ends of the earth.

Jesus *commanded* us to do as much. "Go and make disciples of all nations," He said to His followers (Matthew 28:19). Obedience demands that we go.

Paul the apostle found himself motivated as well by *love*. "Christ's love compels us," he told the Corinthians (2 Corinthians 5:14). The love of God, poured out into his heart by the Holy Spirit (see Romans 5:5), reached out to people who had not heard about the Savior.

At the same time, Paul sees it as a *reasonable* vocation: "We are convinced," he says, "that one died for all, and therefore all died. And he died for all, that those who live should no longer live for themselves but for him who died for them and was raised again" (2 Corinthians 5:14-15).

Our Lord suggested a further motivation when He said, "This gospel of the kingdom will be preached in the whole world as a testimony to all nations, and then the end will come" (Matthew 24:14). Do we long to see the return of Jesus Christ and the ushering in of His millennial reign? Jesus implies it will happen when this gospel of the kingdom has been proclaimed to all nations. In John's vision of heaven he saw Jesus as a slain Lamb, and heard the four "living creatures" and the 24 elders, all bowing prostrate before this Lamb, singing:

> . . . with your blood you purchased men for
>   God
> from every tribe and language and people
>   and nation.
> You have made them to be a kingdom and
>   priests to serve our God,
> and they will reign on the earth.
>
> (Revelation 5:9-10)

Heaven is to be populated with human beings from every tribe and language and people and nation. Will it happen if we do not take the initiative to evangelize these ethnic groups?

But whatever other motives there may be for taking the gospel to the ends of the earth, certainly God's glory is among the highest. A sinner converted to Christ is a majestic spectacle, a display of God's power that makes His reputation highly impressive. It gains the recognition of other people who, in turn, may put their faith in Christ. And the more sinners who are converted to the Savior, the larger the display of the glory of Christ.

What a grand motivation for evangelism and missions!

Missions and the Great Commission

by Peter N. Nanfelt

MAYBE WE HAVE TALKED AND PREACHED too much about the Great Commission. Among some Christians and in some local churches there is a growing feeling that we need to back off a bit. To be perfectly honest, the feeling may be even stronger than that. In some quarters there is actually a rising sense of resentment about anything that has to do with missions.

Why would this be so? Perhaps there are some good reasons. For example, some churches outstanding in their support of missions are no longer significantly impacting their own communities. Is this what Christ intended when He commissioned His church to take the gospel to the world?

Others suggest that a missionary denomination can get out of balance. So much of its effort is going abroad that it no longer can meet its obligations as a church organization. The missionary emphasis, rather than being a clarion call that motivates and mobilizes the constituents, increasingly drains limited resources.

One might also observe that Christians in the non-

Western world now considerably outnumber Christians in the West. Doesn't that mean it is time for some changes? When the New Testament churches in Asia and Europe began to prosper, did they not send support to the mother church in Jerusalem?

We Must Keep Our Perspective

If we think of the Great Commission only as a New Testament command, we can easily lose our perspective. We can become like soldiers amid a hard-fought battle. Their officer tells them to do certain things or engage in certain maneuvers. To the troops, these orders make no sense at all. The embattled soldiers are full of questions. The "why?" questions. And the "how?" questions. And the "wouldn't it be more logical if . . . ?" questions.

The troops have lost sight of the big picture. They forget that the battle in which they are involved is only a small part of the greater war being waged. They may *talk* about the larger war, but most soldiers are focused on their local situation. They do not have a broad understanding of the overall battle. They do not understand how what they are being asked to do can possibly contribute to some worthwhile victory. Similarly, we as Christians can become so consumed by our local situation that we lose sight of the big picture. As a result, we can begin to question the continuing validity of the Great Commission for us. Feelings of resentment toward Christ's command can begin to grow in our hearts and minds. Before we know it, what was once an absolute mandate from our Commander becomes an outdated suggestion that we question and analyze.

God's Plan for Humanity

We have no license to turn a command of Christ into a suggestion. But maybe we do need to talk less about the Great Commission and more about God's greater plan for humanity. We sometimes forget that the Great Commission is simply the New Testament expression of a divine theme woven throughout the Scriptures. Even some of the Great Commission texts in the New Testament reflect this.

Look at Luke 24:36-49, Jesus' post-resurrection meeting with His disciples. After calming the disciples' initial fears, Jesus speaks some very profound truths: "This is what I told you while I was still with you: Everything must be fulfilled that is written about me in the Law of Moses, the Prophets and the Psalms" (24:44). What were "the Law of Moses, the Prophets and the Psalms"? They were the Jewish designation for the entire Old Testament Scriptures.

Luke goes on to say that Jesus "opened their minds so they could understand the Scriptures" (24:45), or the Old Testament. "This is what is written," Jesus told them: "The Christ will suffer and rise from the dead on the third day, and repentance and forgiveness of sins will be preached in his name to all nations, beginning at Jerusalem" (24:46-47).

Jesus linked His Great Commission statement to the entire Old Testament. In fact, He went further than that. Jesus reduced the Old Testament Scriptures to two central themes. The first theme is Jesus Christ Himself: His suffering, death and resurrection. We call it the gospel, the good news. The second theme is the proclamation of the gospel.

Jesus said that this gospel of "repentance and forgiveness of sins will be preached in his name to all nations." Two themes: (1) the gospel and (2) the proclamation of the gospel to the world. Jesus said that this is what the Old Testament Scriptures are all about.

Of Primary Importance

Is this important? Of course it is. As Robert Kurka points out in his exposition of this passage, "World evangelization is not a first-time idea of the resurrected Christ to His church, but rather is an essential thread which unites Genesis to Malachi" (*Completing the Task, Reaching the World for Christ,* Edgar J. Elliston and Steven E. Burns, editors, p. 18). World evangelization was not dreamed up by first-century church leaders. Nor is it a hollow trimuphalism that Christians of more recent times have embraced. According to Jesus Christ Himself, the worldwide proclamation of God's gospel is one of the two major themes of the Bible.

The apostle Paul clearly understood what Jesus had said to His disciples. As he testifies in King Agrippa's court (Acts 26:19-23), Paul stands before the king to defend himself against the charges of Jewish leaders. They had called him a heretic and a troublemaker. Paul relates to King Agrippa his confrontation with the risen Christ on the Damascus road. He tells how he had put his faith in Jesus as the incarnate Son of God. He goes on to relate how he had faithfully preached Jesus Christ to both Jews and Gentiles.

"That," says Paul, "is why the Jews seized me in the temple courts and tried to kill me" (26:21). "But

. . ."—and this is the important point, for Paul goes on to affirm—"I am saying nothing beyond what the prophets and Moses said would happen—that the Christ would suffer and, as the first to rise from the dead, would proclaim light to his own people and to the Gentiles" (26:22-23).

Here are the same two themes to which Jesus had reduced the Old Testament Scriptures: Christ, His suffering, death and resurrection, *and* the proclamation of this message of light to the nations. Paul essentially says the same thing to King Agrippa that Jesus had said to His disciples. He reaffirms the truth that God's plan for world evangelization is at the heart of the Old Testament.

Some Specific References

A review of the Old Testament itself will further underscore this teaching. Go back, for example, to Genesis 3:15. There we find the first clear reference to salvation. God says that the seed of the woman would crush the head of the serpent. We understand this to be a reference to the promised Messiah who would ultimately come from Eve's descendants. He would destroy the devil—an act that would require the Messiah Himself to be severely "bruised" on the cross. Here in the early chapters of the Old Testament the salvation theme is introduced.

Then see what happens just a little further along, in Genesis 12. God calls Abraham and makes an astonishing promise to the patriarch. God says, "All peoples on earth will be blessed through you" (12:3). Here is the second great theme of the Bible, the proclamation of the gospel. It comes through loudly and clearly in these early pages of the Bible. What does God say when He calls Abraham to be the father of the Jewish people? He declares He is God of the Jewish nation that will come from Abraham's loins. But He is also God of the whole world.

Later God repeated this promise to Abraham (Genesis 18:18; 22:18) in an effort to make it absolutely clear to the Jewish people that they had a global responsibility. Through them, all peoples of the world were to hear about God's gospel and be the recipients of His blessing. Paul catches the essence of this truth when he writes, "The Scripture foresaw that God would justify the Gentiles by faith, and announced the gospel in advance to Abraham: 'All nations will be blessed through you' " (Galatians 3:8).

Read through the Old and New Testaments and the global aspect of the divine message is unmistakably clear. The Psalms repeatedly elevate and magnify the God of *all nations*. The prophet Isaiah talks about the testimony of Israel to the *nations*. The story of Jonah is not simply a tale about a whale. It is the account of God's reaching out to the *nations*. The New Testament evangelists write that their gospels of Jesus are for the *nations*. The book of Acts is the account of the early church taking the gospel to the *nations*. Jesus and Paul had it right when they spoke of world evangelization as being the very essence of God's ongoing plan for humankind. It was formulated before the foundation of the world.

What Should We Conclude?

But where does all of this lead us? Jesus implies

that completing God's plan of world evangelization will lead to His return: "This gospel of the kingdom will be preached in the whole world as a testimony to all nations, and then the end will come" (Matthew 24:14).

We are convinced that Jesus will come again. Many of us believe that He could come at any moment. We do not preach it enough. Unlike the early Christians, we do not live with this end-time mentality stamped on our lifestyles. But we believe that Jesus will return. Unfortunately, the long wait has blunted our sense of alertness.

At some time or another, all of us have gone to the airport or the bus or train station to meet an arriving guest. At first we are very attentive, quite sure that our guest will appear at any moment. But if there are announced delays and our alertness has gone unrewarded, we become more lax. We might even slip into the coffee shop for a few moments, feeling quite sure that our guest will not arrive during that brief period.

For two thousand years the Christian church has anticipated Christ's return. That is a long time to wait. It is surprising, really, that the early church was so convinced that Jesus would come back so quickly. Jesus had told His followers the gospel must first be proclaimed in all the world (Matthew 24:14). Did the first-century Christians know what that meant? Were the early church leaders unaware of the expanse of the continents? Did they have no knowledge of the world's population? We cannot fully answer those questions. But if I had lived in the first century and knew *then* what I know *now*, I would probably have had some questions about the immediacy of Christ's return.

More True Today?

But wait a minute. If it was true then that Christ's return had to be delayed until the gospel was preached in the whole world, wouldn't it be even more true today? There are more non-Christians on earth now than ever before in history. In light of this reality, isn't it even less likely that Jesus will appear today than it was in the first century? No, I do not think so.

First, we need to understand that we cannot put God in a box and dictate to Him when Christ can or cannot return. Second, we do not fully understand what Jesus meant when He declared, "This gospel . . . will be preached in the whole world." Did He mean that every single individual will hear the gospel? Did He mean that every people group will hear the gospel? And, if that was His intention, what is God's definition of a people group?

We cannot answer those questions. But we must not be oblivious to the fact that Christ's Great Commission is in the process of being completed.

Over the years I have enjoyed telling about a family experience we had in Indonesia. One day my wife and I and another missionary couple stopped at a restaurant. The other couple and we each had our five-year-old sons along. As we entered the restaurant, the boys spotted a video game. These technological marvels were new to us at the time, but interestingly enough, our five-year-olds knew all about video games. They offered to show us how this one worked if we would provide them with the necessary coins. Having a few minutes to spare, we four adults stood behind the boys as they inserted the coins and began to push the buttons and turn the knobs.

We watched with considerable amazement as flaming rockets flew across the screen and bombs rained down. "Look at this!" we exclaimed. "Did you see that?" Slowly, our two five-year-olds turned around and looked up at us.

"See what?" they asked.

Suddenly we realized that the boys were so short they could not see the big screen above their heads. They had no idea that so much exciting action was taking place. They were just enjoying the sound effects and the fun of pushing the buttons and turning the knobs. Needless to say, they were utterly astounded when we picked them up and let them see what was really going on.

Do We Know What God Is Doing?

Sometimes I think the evangelical church in America is oblivious to what God is doing in the world. In fact, there are multiple evidences that the gospel is being proclaimed to the far corners of the planet as never before. Huge, powerful radio transmitters, some of the largest ever built, broadcast the gospel in hundreds of languages understood by most of the world's people. The Scriptures have now been translated into well over 2,000 languages spoken by 91 percent of the human race. Last year alone, 1.9 billion copies of the Scriptures or Scripture portions were distributed across the world.

Five hundred years ago there was one born-again, Bible-believing Christian in the world for every one hundred non-Christians. Today, although there are more non-Christians overall, the ratio is one born-again believer to less than ten non-Christians. Thirty-five years ago almost 70 percent of the world's Christians were in the Western world. Now 70 percent of the world's Christians are in the non-Western world. Never before in the history of mankind has the gospel been preached so widely and so extensively.

Jesus said that the theme of the Scriptures was the suffering, resurrected Savior and the proclamation of His death and resurrection to the world. He also predicted that this gospel would be preached in all the world and then the end would come. That worldwide proclamation is happening right before our eyes! God is carrying out His divine plan for the human race.

We Are Participants with God

No wonder the Bible ends with such an emphasis on the culmination of God's plan for the world. The Revelation mentions "the nations" 19 times. Seven different times John the writer uses the phrase, "every nation, tribe, people and language," or words very similar.

The two major themes of Scripture come to spectacular fulfillment in the final book of the Bible. The story of salvation is to be told to the whole world. Why? Because it has always been God's will . . .

> *that at the name of Jesus every knee should bow,*
> *in heaven and on earth and under the earth,*
> *and every tongue confess that Jesus Christ is*
> *Lord,*
> *to the glory of God the Father.*
> (Philippians 2:10-11)

With this in mind we can understand the excitement of the apostle John when he wrote,

> After this I looked and there before me was a great multitude that no one could count, from every nation, tribe, people and language, standing before the throne and in front of the Lamb. They were wearing white robes and were holding palm branches in their hands. And they cried out in a loud voice:
>
> "Salvation belongs to our God,
> who sits on the throne,
> and to the Lamb."
>
> (Revelation 7:9-10)

Let's not be like soldiers in the trenches. So often they just focus on the marching orders. They try their best to follow the commands of their officer, but lacking adequate understanding of the overall battle plan, the burden of obedience becomes ever heavier.

We are soldiers of the cross. Our Commanding Officer has shown us the big picture. When we do Great Commission work, we are not involved in a meaningless skirmish. We are participating with God in bringing to fulfillment His plan for the ages.

Missions and the Lostness of Mankind

CHAPTER

4

CHAPTER

4

by Arnold L. Cook

WE OFTEN GO ABOUT OUR CHRIS-
TIAN WORK without the least thought
of our motives. We do things because
they need doing or because that is the way we have
always done them. But motives are important. They
are the fuel that fires the servant of God in ministry.
They *must* be present. And they must be biblical.

The motives that governed the life of the apostle
Paul were especially compelling. Addressing the
Ephesian elders he reminded them: "For three years
I never stopped warning each of you night and day
with tears" (Acts 20:31).

To the Corinthians he confessed, "Woe to me if I
do not preach the gospel!" (1 Corinthians 9:16).
And he wrote to the Romans, "I could wish that I
myself were cursed and cut off from Christ for the
sake of my brothers" (Romans 9:3).

Four Motives

In his second letter to the Corinthians, Paul mentions four motives for persuading men and women
to become Christians. The first is the fear of the

Lord: "Since, then, we know what it is to fear the Lord, we try to persuade men" (5:11).

The second is in 5:14: "Christ's love compels us." Christ in us is not only our hope of glory but also the One who urges us by the Holy Spirit "to seek and to save what was lost" (Luke 19:10).

Second Corinthians 5:17 sets forth the third motive for reaching people: "If anyone is in Christ, he is a new creation." We have no competition! Only Christ can transform the depraved nature of people.

Paul mentions the fourth motive repeatedly in 5:18-20. We have the message that everyone needs. At the core of every interpersonal problem in the world is human conflict. The answer is also universal: reconciliation. And we have been given "the ministry of reconciliation" (5:18).

The first of these four great motives, the fear of the Lord, is missing today in most presentations of the gospel. This phrase brings to our mind judgment, the wrath of God and hell.

What about the eternal destiny of people without Christ? Is a conviction that they are headed for judgment and doom a valid motive for evangelism and missions? I believe that it is. Here are my reasons:

Such motivation is based on biblical truth. In the Old Testament the wrath of God is a common theme. God moved in wrath against individuals such as Moses, Miriam, Aaron and Balaam. Groups of people—the children of Israel, the cities of Sodom and Gomorrah and the enemies of God's people—felt the sting of His wrath. The nations that forgot the Lord were a special target of His displeasure.

The apostle Paul makes frequent references to the

wrath of God. Of the 30 times the term "wrath" is employed throughout the New Testament, 17 of these are found in his writings. Jesus implies God's wrath in John 3:16. He specifically articulates it in 3:36: "Whoever rejects the Son will not see life, for God's wrath remains on him."

A Literal Hell

The fact that hell is a literal place of eternal torment is a terrible truth. It is terrifying. All of our humanism cries out against such a notion.

This kind of a hell can be derived neither inductively nor deductively. For this reason Louis L. King calls it "an article of faith." It comes to us through the revelation of God's Word.

God in His Word gives us several graphic glimpses of hell. The rich man in torment (Luke 16:19-31) is one of them. The place of judgment and the "lake of fire" (Revelation 20:11-15) is another. Hell is described elsewhere in the New Testament as a place of imprisonment, weeping, darkness, eternal punishment, damnation, great pain. It is the place prepared for the devil and his angels.

The eternal damnation of those who are apart from Christ is a neglected truth. It is denied by many theologians of our day. If they address the issue, they tend to draw one of two conclusions: all people will be saved ultimately, or the lost will be annihilated.

Most church-growth writings also neglect this great motivation for reaching people. Even some evangelistic programs have chosen to bypass it. But this current disregard ignores the fact that Christ mentioned hell many more times than He mentioned heaven.

Of some 70 applicants that I have interviewed for ministry, two-thirds testified to being converted as children. Most were apologetic about their experiences, because they felt their motive for trusting in Christ was fear—the fear of being lost and missing heaven.

But I ask, "What is wrong with fearing God?" Scripture says, "The fear of the LORD is the beginning of wisdom" (Proverbs 9:10).

In Church History

Michael Green, discussing evangelistic motivation in the early church, discusses the belief in a literal hell. He concludes: "This lively awareness of the peril of those without Christ persisted as a major evangelistic motive into the second century."

Comparing two great missionary centuries, Carl F. H. Henry states:

> The two centuries of greatest advance of the Christian faith, the first and the nineteenth centuries, were those in which the [reality of the] lostness of [people] without Christ and the desire to save them from a Christless eternity were the strongest.

Leighton Ford reminds us:

> The belief that [people are] lost is far from the only motive for evangelism. There are 1,001 positive reasons for winning [people] to Christ. Yet there is this one great negative, that [they] should

not perish. Take away that and you will cut the very nerve cord of concern.

Another church leader underlines this great motivational truth:

> *It was when I realized that [people] without God were lost now and would be lost forever—even nice folk, even my family and friends—that I vowed I would burn up my one life telling others of the fabulous good news that Jesus brought to our world.*

We must recognize the reality of the condemnation of those who do not know Christ as Savior. Though this is neglected truth, it is biblical. And because this is a terrible truth, it is compelling.

I have copied this prayer in the flyleaf of each of my Bibles to keep me constantly moved with concern for people outside of Christ: "Oh God, may we never get used to hearing the thud of Christless feet on the road to hell."

CHAPTER	Missions and
5	the Kingdom

Missions and the Kingdom

by David P. Jones

YOU'RE NOTHING BUT A RELIGIOUS IM-
PERIALIST and a spiritual colonizer!" The
harsh, angry words of the Brazilian official,
standing in our yard, rang heavily in my ears. How
could this happen? My wife, Judy, and I had spent
months praying and preparing for a church among
the middle-upper class of Brasília, the nation's capital. A divinely arranged appointment had led to an
evangelistic Bible study in the home of a federal
judge. We had seen a breakthrough as several
adults made firm, first-time decisions for Christ.
Two of them were the wife and daughter of my accuser. Even he had made a tentative move toward
the Savior. But as his wife and daughter grew in the
grace and knowledge of Jesus, the official became
increasingly antagonistic. Jealousy hounded him as
his wife looked to us two *gringos* (Judy and me) for
spiritual leadership and discipleship.

Now he stood, his wife in tow, outside our garage,
refusing to enter our home. He waved his hands
angrily in the air as he forbade his wife to attend the
"foreign" church services in our simple, rented hall.

I conceded he had the right to forbid his wife to attend our church. But I also reminded him that the Scriptures warn Christians against "giv[ing] up meeting together" (Hebrews 10:25). Therefore, he could not ban her from attending some good evangelical church.

The man reluctantly accepted the authority of God's Word. Eventually he permitted his wife to joined another church, where she continued to grow in the Lord.

An Honest Reassessment

After the official and his wife left that evening, Judy and I sat down, discouraged and questioning. Were we really "religious imperialists," "spiritual colonizers"? Those charges stung. Despite the fact that we were "foreigners," our years of work in Brazil had eliminated any noticeable accent from our Portuguese. Our church services were much more Brazilian in style than the worship services in North America where we were raised. Our daily conversations and thoughts—even my sermon illustrations—were filled with our Brazilian experiences.

Did this government official and lawyer really think we were trying to impose an imported religion on his countrymen? Did he really think we were trying to establish a religious empire, colonizing the souls of Brazilians? Was that the reason for his anger? No, we concluded. Notwithstanding our foreign origin and residual "gringo-ness," we were not preaching a North American God, nor were we attempting to establish some kind of religious colony. We were proclaiming the gospel of Jesus Christ and the establishment of God's kingdom. So we lifted our heads and hearts in prayer. We asked God to prosper the seed planted in the hearts of this man and his family. Then we started all over to proclaim the kingdom and practice its ethics in our everyday lives.

The Priority Petition

In His Sermon on the Mount, Jesus has much to say about prayer. He tells us to pray thoughtfully and according to God's will, not by vain repetition. His well-known "Lord's Prayer" (Matthew 6:9-13) is a pattern for His followers. His order for prayer begins with adoration, followed by total submission to His will. Then come our "daily bread" petitions, after which we are to confess sin and request protection from the evil one.

What is unique about this prayer is the phrase that follows the opening adoration. We are to pray, "Your kingdom come." The first real request in the prayer is for the Father's kingdom. Before asking for "daily bread" (where most of us begin our prayers), Jesus asks for the "coming" of God's kingdom. The coming of the kingdom refers to its realization, its actuality, its coming into being.

Jesus taught us to pray for the kingdom's coming and for God's will to be done on earth as in heaven. It is apparent, therefore, that He was looking forward to a yet-to-be-realized kingdom on earth. It is apparent also that this kingdom has always been in existence in heaven. The reference to a yet-to-be-established kingdom on earth implies certain far-reaching theological and practical conclusions.

First, this prayer implies that there is another kingdom presently in place. It is a *counter-kingdom,* an alien authority, that presently rules over the earth.

A Usurper Has Wrested Control

Our Heavenly Father is God Almighty, the only divine being in the universe. Nevertheless, this counter-kingdom has a leader who is God's rival. He is a supplanter who has somehow usurped authority and control over this planet God created. This counter-kingdom has a counterfeit king who is variously called "the prince of this world" (John 14:30), "the ruler of the kingdom of the air" (Ephesians 2:2), the "prince of demons" (Matthew 9:34).

A third conclusion from the prayer Jesus gave His disciples is about the *coming kingdom*. It is something to be prayed and worked for. It is a future happening to be anticipated and expected. John the Baptizer preached repentance while proclaiming that the kingdom of heaven was close at hand. He declared that he was not the Messiah, the one who would usher in that kingdom. His job was to "prepare the way for the Lord," to "make straight paths for him" (Matthew 3:1-3).

What John described as his role in preparing for the kingdom parallels the role of missions and the missionary. The man or woman who has received God's call to proclaim the gospel cross-culturally is a kingdom herald. This good news is for all people everywhere. It states that the Father of our Lord Jesus Christ is the true God. His kingdom is the rightful one over earth. This message of salvation defines who are citizens of the kingdom and how a person can become one. The evangel of the missionary is to be "supra-cultural"—above all cultures, customs, human creeds and codes of conduct.

The Kingdom's Ruler

The apostolic message is simple: God is King of the universe, Lord Almighty, Creator and Preserver of everything. Just as Jesus did, the missionary declares God to be the "Father in Heaven." In other words, He is Progenitor of us all, the only One who has all authority and power over all people everywhere. God is in heaven and we are here on earth, which He made for our proper place of habitation and activity. He made us for His glory and pleasure. He made us to be like Him, as loving children. He made us to know and love Him willingly. He made us to have abundant, meaningful, satisfying lives. This is His "will" that He desires "to be done on earth as it is in heaven."

But wait! What has happened? How did this sick, sadistic, selfish world that we know and live in come to be? The 21st century apostle, just as Paul in the 1st century, must announce the other side of the good news. Satan is the ruler of this counter-realm of pain, suffering and sin. Humankind was deceived by the serpent. Adam and Eve disobeyed God's rule and rebelled. Unwittingly, they alienated themselves from their perfect environment. They became separated from their Creator, estranged from each other and disaffected with themselves.

The world as we know it is now under the control of Satan, the rival ruler of this world. His counter-kingdom is diametrically opposed to God and His will. While not equal to God's kingdom in power and authority, it is pervasive and powerful over all the earth. From the beginning, the devil has used the "bait and switch" technique. "You don't need God; do your own thing. Live it up—with gusto!" Just as in the Garden, the counter-kingdom message is one of initial deception and final destruction. Good is falsified; evil is disguised. Satan purports to offer love, freedom and purpose in life. But once people are taken in by this alluring offer, they find instead hate, slavery and meaninglessness. Such is sin's forbidden fruit.

An Example from Brazil

Jardim das Palmeiras (Garden of the Palms) has an idyllic name. But reality paints quite a different picture. This *bairro* in the city of Porto Alegre is populated by the urban poor. They are land invaders who have taken up "squatters' rights," living in squalor in this stronghold of spiritism. Yet, God sent a young Christian couple to move into the neighborhood. Through their witness, their landlady and her family came to Christ. There was a confrontation between the spiritist medium, who weekly frequented the landlady's home, and the Christian couple. It resulted in the defeat of the "spirits," who would not manifest themselves due to the couple's warfare praying. Soon the Christian couple began to hold weekly Bible studies in their home. They also had Sunday afternoon open-air meetings for the neighborhood children. Within just a few weeks, these street kids ceased their daily rock fights, which previously had been their after-school activity. A short time later, our mission helped this couple build a portable chapel in the backyard of the landlady's home. Within weeks, the spiritist medium who lived next door, moved out.

"I can't stay here any longer," the medium declared with disgust. "Those crazy believers won't let the spirits come down here anymore!"

Jardim das Palmeiras still is not a garden, and there are no palms there. But the gospel has penetrated that little piece of Satan's real estate, and God's kingdom has brought freedom and life to many.

The Kingdom's Rule

John Milton described humankind's fall as *Paradise Lost*. He was accurate. There was perfection in the Garden. God and humanity were at peace in a loving, personal communion. The first family lived in perfect harmony with its environment.

The best summation of kingdom conduct and character, as first seen in the Garden, is found in the Sermon on the Mount (Matthew 5-7). This "kingdom constitution" describes how the "happy kingdom people" are to live. In the first of the "beatitudes," Jesus said that the "humble" and the "poor in spirit" are the true possessors of heaven's kingdom. He teaches a rule of humility, of self-sacrificing love. He talks of a life dedicated to the combat of the counter-kingdom's rule. It is a life that will seek to imitate the conduct and character of "the sons of God."

The missionary takes a message of freedom from sin, fear and evil to cultures and peoples dominated by Satan's rule of darkness. This "foreigner" seeks to become as much as possible like the people he or she seeks to reach with the gospel. He or she takes on their customs, learns their language, eats their food. However, this friendly invader is also a bringer of innovation. The missionary doesn't seek to wipe out the indigenous people's culture and way of life. The missionary message, however, that comes from a transcendent, all-powerful God inevitably will clash with much in that culture. Throughout the history of missions, cultures have been powerfully impacted and age-old customs have been changed as the gospel freed people from evil's bonds. In India, for example, *suttee,* the practice of widow-burning, was wiped out as the gospel penetrated the culture.

Jesus came as the God-Man to conquer the power and penalty of sin over the human race. He came to free humanity to love and serve God, to do good to neighbors. Cross-cultural evangelization takes the proclamation of peace to the untold and the unreached. This brings predictable conflict with Satan, his kingdom and his followers.

He Refused to Bow to God's Rule

As I drove up to the simple, plank-walled home in a working-class neighborhood of Curitiba, Paraná, I heard a bloodcurdling scream. It was followed by a loud crash and the sound of shattering dishes. I was responding to a frantic phone call from one of our church members. She asked me if I might help her calm Laertes, her drunken, demonized husband. He was threatening to kill her and her daughter and destroy their house.

I hurried into the small building and witnessed a scene of chaos and fear. Their six-year-old daughter cowered in the corner. The wife cringed as her husband systematically beat his head against the wall. For more than two hours, I alternately tried to calm the man and rebuke the evil spirits within him. Finally an inhuman voice rose up from somewhere within the man, laughing and roaring.

"I won't come out of him," the voice said. "He is mine, and I don't have to leave. I'm not finished tormenting him. And I'm not done with giving *you* a bad time either!"

That was just one of several power encounters I witnessed in the man's life. He recognized the truth of the gospel and believed intellectually that Jesus Christ was Lord and God. But he refused to accept Him as Lord and Savior of his life.

"I don't want any god in my life," he told me. "Neither Jesus nor Satan. I want to be my own boss."

I reminded him that he already had a lord in his life—Satan. Only the power of Jesus Christ, God's Son, was strong enough to free him from the control of the demonic servants of Satan. Laertes refused to bow to Christ and gain freedom and eternal life. About a year later, he died as a result of his demon-driven alcohol addiction. His little daughter watched him suffocate to death.

Laertes was not destroyed because the power of God's kingdom is inferior to Satan's. He died because he refused to become a willing and obedient believer in Jesus and a citizen of God's kingdom. I did not bring him an "imperialistic Yankee" gospel. I brought him the message given by Almighty God, recorded in His Word by Middle-Eastern Jews and Mediterranean Gentiles. It is a communication that belongs to no particular race or nationality. It is for "whoever will." Laertes simply refused to bow to the kingdom commands.

Kingdom Citizenship

When Jesus opened the scroll to Isaiah's prophecy (Matthew 4:12-17), He read,

> *The people living in darkness*
> *have seen a great light;*
> *on those living in the land of the shadow*
> *of death*
> *a light has dawned.* (4:16)

Matthew succinctly adds: "From that time on Jesus began to preach, 'Repent, for the kingdom of heaven is near.' "

Matthew saw Jesus as a great Light penetrating to the slaves of Satan's kingdom. He coupled that prophetic word with a command to repentance. This is the order of the "naturalization process." It is through turning to the light and away from the darkness that a person becomes a citizen of the kingdom of God.

Repentance means abandoning the way one was, and making a 180-degree turn. One receives "kingdom citizenship" by the new birth, as Jesus explained to Nicodemus in John 3. The natural man or woman, dead in transgressions and sins, must be born again by God's Spirit. And whoever believes in Jesus will have eternal life. It must be understood and accepted, however, that Jesus is the only "way." Not just any old way will do. To become a citizen of God's kingdom of light, one must approach God through His only Son, Jesus Christ. He is "the way and the truth and the life" (John 14:6). He is the only approach to the Father.

Jesus demands exclusive allegiance. In addition, a person must recognize his or her sinfulness. Humanity stands justly condemned by God. Rousseau's "noble savage" is a myth. The primitive pagan, untouched in the remote recesses of our planet, lives in fear and depravation. He or she rejects the light of God's creative hand, worshiping the creation and the idols of his or her own making. For this the pagan stand guilty and subject to God's wrath (Romans 1:18-20). The internal voice of conscience speaks of right and wrong to people everywhere. Yet they continue to kill, steal, lie and take their neighbor's wife. The heathen are lost, but not because they haven't heard the gospel. They are lost and condemned because they are sinners, as are all people, whether living in a primitive jungle or walking the sophisticated streets of Paris.

The result of humanity's universal sinfulness is condemnation and eternal death. The destiny of all sinners, whether possessors of great or little light, is hell, which is real and forever. The "bad news" of the gospel is that sin's salary is eternal darkness and death, separation from God and perennial punishment. The "good news" declares that the "gift of God is eternal life through Jesus Christ our Lord" (Romans 6:23). One of the driving motivations of missions comes from an acceptance of these truths. The church is compelled to take the message of heaven's kingdom to those bound in the kingdom of darkness. There is simply no other way of forgiveness and freedom from sin.

The Kingdom's Coming

On the night of His resurrection, Jesus stated that

"repentance and forgiveness of sins will be preached in his name to all nations (*ethnoi*/peoples), beginning at Jerusalem. You are witnesses of these things" (Luke 24:47-48). Jesus has told us to preach His gospel to all people in every place and to make disciples of all people groups, baptizing them and teaching them. That is a concise summary of the missionary's message of the kingdom.

The kingdom comes into being when its citizens communicate the gospel of peace as witnesses to all the world. It comes as they seek to reach the unrighteous, the unreached and the unredeemed. As people hear this message, believe it, repent of their sin and follow Jesus exclusively, they become new subjects of God's kingdom. World evangelization is the heart and lungs, the blood and breath of the Body of Christ. Without this dimension of global outreach, the church will die.

Early in 1995, the seed planted more than a decade before in the life of that Brasilia official and lawyer, now retired, began to take root. His wife had continued faithful to Christ, but he had wandered, living in sin, refusing the truth of the gospel. Now, so many years later, while in his old office, he cried out to God.

"God, you must help me. I can't continue to live like this. It's killing me. Please reveal yourself and your truth to me—today!"

That night, he opened a Christian magazine on his wife's bedside table and read of the miraculous healing of a woman in Brasilia who had been declared dead and came back to life. His first reaction was one of scorn. But immediately he seemed to sense that this was the sign he had asked for from God. The next day, he visited the lady featured in the magazine and asked her what had happened. She gladly documented the miracle of healing in her life. Humbly the man bowed his head and asked her to pray for him. He repented of his sinfulness, of his obstinate unbelief and his ungodly lifestyle. Soon he was baptized and became an active church member. Within a few months, he was credentialed as an evangelist and began to preach to the middle-upper class people of his city. Today, he is pastoring a church meeting in his former law office.

No Spiritual Switzerland

Once again the kingdom of God has proven mightier than Satan's rule. The good seed of the gospel, planted by one, watered by another and brought to fruition by the Holy Spirit, has resulted in the salvation of many, the establishment of a church and the extension of God's kingdom.

In this battle between two kingdoms, there is no spiritual Switzerland. Either we are actively serving the King of kings, or we are citizens of the counter-kingdom. God is calling His church to enlist in His world-witness army, to engage the enemy in the power of the Spirit, and to get involved in the work of the kingdom. He expects us to commit all that we have and are to proclaim the truth of the gospel.

Only God's kingdom is eternal. Let us pray, as Jesus prayed, for that kingdom to come. Let us work for His heavenly will to be done on earth. Let us invest our lives and our resources in His kingdom work.

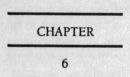

CHAPTER

6

Missions and the Uniqueness of Christ

by H. Robert Cowles

"SOLA SCRIPTURA!" ASSERTED MARTIN LUTHER to a 16th-century church mired in ritual and carnality. Luther was convinced that *Scripture alone* was the infallible source of Christian faith and teaching. All church doctrine and policy must conform to the "sure rule of God's Word."

Today among Luther's Bible-believing Protestant progeny, a new issue has raised its head. Is Christ Jesus *uniquely* the Savior? Will a person who refuses to bow to Him in this life have another chance later? What about those who have never heard of Jesus?

Thinking What Once Was Unthinkable

A generation ago, to suppose there might be salvation apart from Jesus Christ was unthinkable—at least in evangelical circles. It was also unthinkable that people would be given a "second notice" post mortem. Not so anymore. Today declared evangelicals are expressing those very thoughts.

Their motives are altruistic. They are concerned for a world gone awry. They desire what God desires—

the salvation of all people. In a world of billions they see a church of only millions. They question that a merciful God could possibly condemn so many to eternal punishment. Especially those who have had no adequate opportunity to hear of Jesus Christ. The specter of a real hell and unending torment has caused them to seek loopholes.

But the issue is crucial for the very unreached people about whom they are concerned. If their opinion prevails, it will have a chilling effect on world missions. Why strain to reach the last tribe with the good news of Jesus Christ if God has a Plan B?

Not a New Concept

This may be a new issue in evangelical circles, but it is not a new concept. There have always been those who suppose a loving God will not send sinners to hell. There have always been those who argue that all religions lead to God. What is new is for so-called evangelicals to be saying such things.

Granted their motives are high and their concern for lost people is deep and genuine. But the Scriptures are on our side, not theirs. We must uphold the sure rule of God's Word. If those who question God's Word prevail, we can write off missions as a failed cause. It's that black and white.

God's Word declares there is but one way to God, and that is through Jesus Christ (John 14:6). "Whoever does not believe stands condemned already because he has not believed in the name of God's one and only Son" (John 3:18). This believing or trusting in Christ must be done in this life, for after death is the judgment (Hebrews 9:27).

It is time to lift a new banner to fly beside Luther's. This one reads *SOLO SALVATOR!*—The *only* Savior. The Lord Jesus Christ alone can save. Outside of Jesus Christ there is no salvation.

Bible Illiterates

Not all the questioning is from academe. Ask members of the "thirty-something" generation in your church if God will consign to hell a person who never heard of Christ. Ask them if Muslims or Buddhists who sincerely follow what light they have will be eternally lost. Their answers may astonish you.

For at least two generations, North Americans have been growing up with minimal or no exposure to the Scriptures. Certainly they haven't had it in the public schools. And few of them have had it in church or Sunday school. Even Christian families rarely attempt any sort of systematic Bible study.

As a result, many younger people, though they may go to church, know little of what the Bible teaches. And in truth, they don't especially care. Searching for a code of beliefs is not their purpose for going to church. They go to get a "lift." They go to be ministered to, and to minister. They go to associate with their friends. Beliefs are incidental— somewhere out on the fringes of their thinking. Their "theology," such as it is, is a mishmash of garden-variety morality and relativistic reasoning. Not always does the pulpit help them sort out fact from fiction.

If someone confronts them with weighty speculations concerning eternal issues, they respond from the heart.

• Will a God of love condemn sinners to eternal fire?

• What about those who have never heard of Jesus? Will He condemn them?

• What about sincere Muslims? or Buddhists? Will they end up in hell?

"No to all three!" they reply after briefly consulting their emotions. "Our God is a God of *love!*"

Second-Chance Safety Net

That sounds like a point-blank denial that Jesus is the only Savior. But not necessarily. We want to be fair both to biblically weak Christians who vote with their emotions and to scholarly types who have thought deeply about these questions.

By no means do all who answer "No" to the above questions intend to bypass Jesus Christ and His blood atonement. Quite the contrary. With them it is a *when* issue. In their theology, physical death is not the cut-off point. They envision a second-chance scenario after physical death. Those who rejected Christ on earth—or who never heard of Him—will be given another opportunity after physical death to decide. In the case of Christ rejecters, presumably it will be under more persuasive circumstances.

Looking, therefore, at the big picture, we find ourselves confronted by three questions:

1. *Jesus Christ is the Savior from* what?
2. *Jesus Christ is the Savior* when?
3. *Jesus Christ is the Savior with* whom else?

We will take up the questions in that order, then relate them to missions (the theme of this book).

Finally we shall draw an appropriate conclusion.

Jesus Christ Is the Savior from *What*?

If you said, "Jesus Christ is the Savior from sin," you are right. If you said from something else, for example, hell, you are partly right.

The Scriptures are clear. The angel of the Lord said to Joseph, the virgin Mary's fiancé: "You are to give him the name Jesus, because he will save his people from their sins" (Matthew 1:21). Paul declared, "Here is a trustworthy saying that deserves full acceptance: Christ Jesus came into the world to save sinners—of whom I am the worst" (1 Timothy 1:15). These and many other Scriptures indicate that Jesus' death on the cross was to save us from our *sins*.

We have come to regard sin far too lightly. God doesn't. He is holy (sin-free) in the absolute sense, and He commanded even the Old Testament Israelites likewise to be holy (Leviticus 11:44-45; 19:2). It is so in the church era, too. "Once you were alienated from God and were enemies in your minds because of your evil behavior," Paul told the Colossians. "But now he has reconciled you by Christ's physical body through death to present you holy in his sight, without blemish and free from accusation" (Colossians 1:21-22). To the Thessalonians Paul says, "May God himself, the God of peace, sanctify you through and through. May your whole spirit, soul and body be kept blameless at the coming of our Lord Jesus Christ" (1 Thessalonians 5:23).

Only when we understand how repulsive sin is to God can we appreciate what Jesus did to save us from it. Christians seize on the notion that we are innocent until our confrontation by Jesus Christ. At that point, we are saved if we receive Him and lost if we refuse or reject Him. Yes and no. We must receive the Lord Jesus Christ into our lives in order to be saved. But we were already "dead in [our] transgressions and sins" (Ephesians 2:1), whether or not we encountered Jesus. As Ronald H. Nash succinctly puts it, "Rejecting Christ is not a condition for being lost. We are lost already." (*Is Jesus the Only Savior?* [Grand Rapids: Zondervan, 1994] p. 155.)

The Bible introduces us to a glorious fact: "When [we] were dead in [our] sins and in the uncircumcision of [our] sinful nature, God made [us] alive with Christ. He forgave us all our sins, having canceled the written code, with its regulations, that was against us and that stood opposed to us; he took it away, nailing it to the cross" (Colossians 2:13-14). Jesus Christ is our Savior from *sin!*

Jesus Christ Is the Savior *When?*

Sin has consequences, the chief of them being hell for the finally impenitent. Whatever its reality, hell is clearly a destination to be avoided. If we fail to take the necessary measures in this life, can we expect a second chance in the next? What about those who never had opportunity to encounter Christ? Surely *they* deserve not a second chance but a *first* chance to hear the good news of a Savior. They deserve opportunity to receive Him into their lives.

If God indeed has a Plan B, the Scriptures make no hint of it. Not even in that difficult-to-interpret passage about Jesus preaching to the disobedient antediluvian "spirits in prison" (1 Peter 3:19). Surely that reference was an opportune point for God to unveil any back-up plan He might have for saving people after death.

Quite the opposite, the Bible is firm that *this* life constitutes our probation. The decisions we make, or do not make, now set the course for our future after death. "Man is destined to die once, and after that to face judgment" (Hebrews 9:27), I repeat.

The apostle John equates divine love with the divine presence within us. "In this way," he says, "love is made complete among us so that we will have confidence on the day of judgment" (1 John 4:17). Like Peter, John offers no after-death opportunity to make up for negligence in the present life.

Neither did Jesus. "A time is coming," Jesus declares, "when all who are in their graves will hear [the Son of God's] voice and come out—those who have done good will rise to live, and those who have done evil will rise to be condemned" (John 5:28-29). Jesus offers no hint of a post mortem reconciliation prior to the judgment.

When is Jesus the Savior? Now. "Now is the time of God's favor, now is the day of salvation" (2 Corinthians 6:2).

The person who anticipates a second chance after this life ends has put off the decision too long.

Jesus Christ is the Savior with *Whom Else?*

By this point the answer should be apparent. No one but Jesus Christ can save us. He is uniquely the Savior, the only Savior.

"There is one God and one mediator between God and men, the man Christ Jesus, who gave himself as a ransom for all men" (1 Timothy 2:5-6). *Solo Salvator!*

All religions do *not* lead to God. Jesus declares, "I am the way and the truth and the life. No one comes to the Father except through me" (John 14:6). *Solo Salvator!*

"He who has the Son has life; he who does not have the Son of God does not have life" (1 John 5:12). It's that simple. "No one who denies the Son has the Father" (1 John 2:23). *Solo Salvator!*

Such affirmations are not well received by Hindus, Buddhists, Shintoists, Muslims, Mormons. Not even by all Christians. Some of these religions go farther back in time than Christianity. All of them—and others—are well-established, well-recognized.

That much we concede. Neither dare we be arrogant in our attitude. But we cannot deny God's Word. He first said it: "No other Mediator." "No other Way." "No other Name." If we are talking about ways to approach God, we really need to let Him make the decision. God has done so. The Way is Jesus Christ. He is the *only* way. Not Confucius. Not the virgin Mary. Not Muhammad. Not Joseph Smith. Not Mary Baker Eddy. Jesus Christ is the *only* way to God. The *only* way. The *only* way.

Blood on Our Hands

When we come to believe really, truly that Jesus is the only way to God, our missionary program can expect a revolution. We will begin to pray for missions in a new way. Missionary money will begin to flow again. Workers will step forward, saying, "Send *me!*" Here in our own land, too, we will stop playing church and get serious about evangelizing the lost.

And that brings up another question—one that we too often overlook. We grant that those who have never heard of Jesus deserve such an opportunity. But is it God's fault that they have not had that chance? Whom did God commission to tell them? Read the New Testament record if you are in doubt:

> *Then Jesus came to [His followers] and said, . . . "Go and make disciples of all nations."*
> (Matthew 28:18-19)

> *[Jesus] said to [His followers], "Go into all the world and preach the good news to all creation."*
> (Mark 16:15)

> *[Jesus] told [His followers], "This is what is written: The Christ will suffer and rise from the dead on the third day, and repentance and forgiveness of sins will be preached in his name to all nations, beginning at Jerusalem. You are witnesses of these things."* (Luke 24:46-48)

> *Again Jesus said, "Peace be with you! As the Father has sent me, I am sending you."*
> (John 20:21)

> *[Jesus] said to [His apostles]: . . . "You will receive power when the Holy Spirit comes on you; and you will be my witnesses in Jerusalem, and in all Judea and Samaria, and to the ends of the earth."* (Acts 1:7-8)

It Is Not God's Fault

It is not God's fault that after two thousand years the world is yet unevangelized. The blame rests squarely at the church's door.

Jesus issued the command. The apostles set the example. And for more than two centuries the progress was phenomenal. What happened to stop the advance?

For one thing, the persecution of Christians ended. The Christian faith took on respectability. Everybody wanted to climb aboard the bandwagon. The church became at ease and complacent.

There was a second problem. Controversy. Doctrinal disputes. Outright heresies. The church became so busy defending its teachings that it had neither time nor interest to fulfill Jesus' Great Commission.

There was a third problem. Worldliness. All those people who joined up when Christianity became popular brought their pagan trappings with them. The pure gospel got mixed with idolatry and worldly ways.

God has given the church one commission. As the second millennium of the Christian era plays out, we are closer than ever before to true world evangelization. Already 11 percent of the world's people are Bible-believing Christians, says Ralph D. Winter, director of the U.S. Center for World Mission. Dr. Winter defines "Bible-believing Christians" as "those people who read, believe and obey the Bible—whether or not they are as active as they ought to be in helping out with world evangelization."

We Are Winning the War!

Winter goes on to report: "Christianity is by far the fastest growing global religion—if what is measured is Christianity's most significant type of growth—the growth in the number of those truly believing. . . . The kingdom of Christ is expanding . . . at over three times the rate of world population growth."

Statistics like that should cause every true Christian to shout for joy! We're winning! World evangelization by A.D. 2000 is not as far-fetched as we may have supposed.

Jesus declared: "This gospel of the kingdom will be preached in the whole world as a testimony to all nations, and then the end will come" (Matthew 24:14). How much more should those words motivate us today, with the long-anticipated Consummation almost in sight!

Now is the time for the church of Jesus Christ to press on in obedience to the Master's command. Jesus is the only Savior. Never has our world been in greater need of Him. Now is the accepted time.

Forward!

<table>
<tr><td>CHAPTER

7</td><td># Missions and Worship

by Rockwell L. Dillaman</td></tr>
</table>

S UPPOSE YOU AND I WERE PLAYING A game of word association. And suppose I instructed you to write down the first words that came to your mind upon hearing the term *missions*. What entries would you make on your list? "Go"? "Lost"? "Give"? "Obedience"? "Pray"? "Sacrifice"?

How about "worship"? Would "worship" be included in your responses?

At Antioch, where the first missionaries answered the call of the Holy Spirit, worship was very much a part of the picture:

> *While they were worshiping the Lord and fasting, the Holy Spirit said, "Set apart for me Barnabas and Saul for the work to which I have called them." So after they had fasted and prayed, they placed their hands on them and sent them off.*
> *The two of them, sent on their way by the Holy Spirit, went down to Seleucia and sailed from there to Cyprus.* (Acts 13:2-4)

I grew up in an intentionally missionary church. I

vividly recall what seemed to me to be an endless series of exhortations to "go, give and pray!" Many a service consisted of stories of great personal sacrifice. These meetings concluded (though never soon enough for me!) with repeated calls to personal obedience. Those were difficult services for my friends and me. We wanted to enjoy life, and signing on for sacrifice wasn't a part of our agenda. Rather than singing "Pass me not, O gentle Savior," we were praying that God would indeed pass us by! (At least, when it came to missionary service.)

Some years later, I personally encountered God's grace and subsequently sensed God's call to pastoral ministry. But I must confess that the term *missions* continued to evoke images of sacrificial obedience rather than images of worship. When I preached on missions, I did what I had been taught to do. I described the lostness of humankind. I emphasized the responsibility resting on God's people. I left my congregation feeling as if thousands would perish without Christ if they did not respond. It was a call to a great cause, accomplished only at great cost. Regrettably, I did not share what I now recognize to be a gracious invitation to a life of true spiritual freedom—a life most authentically initiated and nurtured in the context of worship.

Duty Is of Relatively Recent Origin

In his book *Pentecost and Missions,* Henry Boer makes an astute observation. The view of evangelism as first and foremost a Christian duty is no older than the 19th century. Prior to that, the church's driving force behind evangelism was simple enthusiasm. There was an inner excitement to share Christ with neighbors and friends. People's joy in discovering new life and hope in Jesus was something they wanted to communicate.

Recent surveys indicate a declining missionary vision among North American churches. Missionaries are hard to find. Missionary funding has tapered off. Has the church lost its sense of hope and excitement nurtured by worship? Has it embraced instead a paradigm of duty and legalistic responsibility? Worse, has world evangelization become a matter of impulse and manipulated guilt trips? If so, do we have any basis for assuming that this "obligation" approach is either acceptable to God or a more effective way to evangelize humankind?

Critically Important Truths

The account of the church in Antioch (Acts 13) demonstrates a number of critically important truths for us. Included among them is the revelation that the fulfillment of the Great Commission requires two things.

First, it requires local assemblies that move in the Spirit and are thereby able to disciple their members in the Spirit-led life. These churches must recognize and receive the prophetic voice of the Spirit. They must identify and confirm those whom the Spirit desires to set apart. They must send forth such missionaries, not only with appropriate ceremony, but with substantive, ongoing support.

Second, it requires called-out people who likewise take their cues from the Spirit. These members are thereby empowered to recognize His call and to discern His voice from the voices of the flesh. They will respond to God's call with gladness. They will continue in mission, by faith, amid the inevitable difficulties and satanic attacks. Let either of these two components be absent, and the entire endeavor is jeopardized.

Missions Requires a Healthy Church

Whenever we commit ourselves to the missionary mandate we are making an assumption. We assume the church is healthy enough to respond in an appropriate fashion. Often that is not the case. Missions is the activity of the Holy Spirit through the church. The record of history makes it quite clear that the church often forsakes the leading of the Spirit. It substitutes instead the activities of the flesh, framed by tradition.

A.W. Tozer recognized this dynamic. It led him to make this thought-provoking observation:

> In the early church, if the Holy Spirit had suddenly withdrawn, 90 percent of what was taking place would have ceased immediately, and everyone would have known He was gone. In the modern church, if the Holy Spirit were to suddenly withdraw, 90 percent of what takes place would continue, and hardly anyone would know that He had left.

The same Holy Spirit who initiates and empowers authentic missions has been sent to make us worshipers. Jesus calls them worshipers "in Spirit and in truth" (John 4:24). The same Spirit inspired Luke to write his account of the Antioch church. The Spirit intentionally led Luke to begin the account with this notation: "While they were worshiping the Lord and fasting . . ." (Acts 13:2). Have we overlooked in these verses a linkage between worship and missions? If so, and if we insist on *un*linking what the New Testament links, how will we succeed? Anything the Spirit deems worthy of mention is worthy of our attention!

In recent years, by God's grace, I have come to better understand the linkage between worship and missions. But first God helped me better understand the linkage between worship and the release of God's power and provision. In the last 10 years I have seen people healed without prayer, saved without preaching, convinced without argument. I have seen them divinely delivered from demonic attack when all else failed. All of this resulted from their entering an atmosphere where God was "inhabit[ing] the praises of Israel" (Psalm 22:3, KJV). As I began to search the Scriptures, I wondered how I could have missed something so biblical for so long!

God's Power Is Released When We Worship

Woven throughout the fabric of God's Word is a consistent correlation between worship and the release of God's power. Jonah is one example. When the reluctant patriot and defiant prophet stopped his pouting and began praising, he was delivered from the great fish (Jonah 2:9-10). Paul and Silas, early missionaries of the church, provide another example. In that filthy, vermin-infested prison in Philippi, they began to worship and praise God. Their sacred concert literally brought the house down (Acts 16:25-26)!

But the clearest and most dynamic example of this phenomenon is in the Old Testament. The account begins with Jehoshaphat and the nation of Judah confronted by a hostile military alliance bent on their destruction. Their response to this predicament would seem utterly foolish to any military strategist today. But to say it was effective would be a gross understatement.

Confronted with possible annihilation, the king and his people bowed down and worshiped the Lord (2 Chronicles 20:18). Then some of the Levites "praised the LORD . . . with very loud voice" (20:19). And

> Jehoshaphat appointed men to sing to the LORD
> and to praise him for the splendor of his holiness
> as they went out at the head of the army, saying:

> "Give thanks to the LORD,
>   for his love endures forever." (20:21)

The Hebrew word for praise in this verse is *yadah*. It means to praise with the movement of the hands. Imagine being one of those men leading the army into battle! The praises of God were upon their lips and their hands were lifted toward the heavens. The enemy must have heard them while they were yet at a distance. With hands extended above their heads and moving, they would be in a position of extreme vulnerability. I have never been one to dehumanize biblical characters. Had I been a part of that singing troupe, I would have been praising God with dry mouth and quivering hands! No one had ever won a battle by worship alone.

"Now for the Rest of the Story"

Well, as news commentator Paul Harvey would say, "Now for the rest of the story." But you know it!

> As they began to sing and praise, the LORD set ambushes against the men of Ammon and Moab and Mount Seir who were invading Judah, and they were defeated. The men of Ammon and Moab rose up against the men from Mount Seir to destroy and annihilate them. After they finished slaughtering the men from Seir, they helped to destroy one another.
> When the men of Judah came to the place that overlooks the desert and looked toward the vast army, they saw only dead bodies lying on the ground; no one had escaped. (20:22-24)

It was a battle won without the use of sword or bow or spear! All would recognize this as a miracle. But we must also see here an illustration of an enduring spiritual reality. Worship and praise facilitate a release of God's power.

Psalm 149 is a Psalm of praise. In it we read:

> May the praise of God be in their mouths
>   and a double-edged sword in their hands,
> to inflict vengeance on the nations
>   and punishment on the peoples,
> to bind their kings with fetters,
>   their nobles with shackles of iron,
> to carry out the sentence written
>   against them.
>   This is the glory of all his saints.
> Praise the LORD. (149:6-9)

In those verses God couples praise and the Word (the double-edged sword of Hebrews 4:12) with spiritual warfare and the binding of His enemies. There is the same linkage in Psalm 8:2, where a worshiping David observes,

> *From the lips of children and infants*
> *   you have ordained praise*
> *because of your enemies,*
> *   to silence the foe and the avenger.*

Missions Is Spiritual Warfare

Missions is not only the activity of the Spirit. It is also spiritual warfare. It is a power encounter. On one side are those who are "strong in the Lord and in his mighty power" (Ephesians 6:10). On the opposing side are "the rulers, . . . the authorities, . . . the powers of this dark world and . . . the spiritual forces of evil in the heavenly realms" (6:12). If we are to succeed in this warfare we must avail ourselves of every spiritual weapon, including worship.

I need to note that the purpose of worship is not to defeat spirit adversaries. It is not to enlist people in world evangelism. Worship is to praise and glorify God. He alone must be the center and focus of our worship. Our objective is to show forth His worth, to stand in His presence with love, awe and humility. But in the act of worshiping God, we experience a multitude of God's blessings and benefits. So, too, does the worshiping assembly. Let me suggest seven benefits that accrue to the worshiping church.

1. God's Power Is Released

First, as we have already noted, worship and praise

result in a release of God's power and provision. Can any church be an effective reproducing and sending community without the power of God? To ask the question is to answer it. God's power must be manifest in its message, its motives, its methods, its mentors and its members. Jesus clearly established the link between power and missions in some of His final instructions to His disciples. Before commencing their missionary work, the disciples were to wait in Jerusalem until they were "clothed with power from on high" (Luke 24:49).

2. Our Love for God Is Sustained

Corporate worship nourishes and sustains our love for God as we focus upon His attributes and His actions. The first and greatest commandment is not "Go and make disciples of all nations . . ." (Matthew 28:19) but "Love the Lord your God . . ." (Matthew 22:37). If we attempt to fulfill the Great Commission without practicing the greatest commandment, we will only produce great commotion. We will wear out the saints without winning the lost.

I love to quote Vance Havner, who had the capacity to capture a great truth in very few words. Havner said, "The primary requirement for missions is not love for souls but love for Jesus." When Jesus was commissioning Peter, He didn't ask Peter if he loved sheep. He asked, "Do you truly love me?" (John 21:15). Jesus knew that anything less than or other than love for Him would not sustain Peter in the mission God had set before him. This is not to say that Peter didn't love people. When you love God you will grow to love what God loves, and God dearly loves "the world" (John 3:16). But love for God is the foundation. An assembly weak in its love for God will prove incapable of being an "Antioch" church.

3. Our Faith in God Is Strengthened

Corporate worship nurtures an attitude of trust in God. "Enter [the LORD's] gates with thanksgiving / and his courts with praise," the psalmist exhorts us (Psalm 100:4). These words are commonly quoted without reference to the important concept found in verse 3: "We are his people, the sheep of his pasture." When the two pictures are combined, we see sheep entering the courts of the Lord. That only occurred when the sheep were about to be sacrificed. Could the Holy Spirit be seeking to reveal to us an important linkage that we easily overlook? As we present ourselves to God as living sacrifices, our praises will enhance our ability to trust God with our lives.

He is the God who gave aging Abraham a son, who exalted imprisoned Joseph to a princely position. He is the God who opened the Red Sea before a seemingly doomed people, who miraculously poured out water from a desert rock, who engineered Israelite victories against better-armed foes. He preserved three young Hebrews in a blazing furnace and closed the mouths of lions to spare Daniel's life.

As we praise this mighty God, we can entrust our beloved children to Him when He calls them to be contemporary Barnabases or Pauls. And when those sons and daughters encounter the enemy, worship creates a determined confidence that God is good, no matter what happens.

4. Our Focus Shifts from Self to God

Corporate worship shifts our focus from self and

self-interest by fixing our attention on God and His purposes. When the psalmist said, "Glorify the LORD with me," he was calling others to join him in "magnify[ing]" (KJV) God. The virgin Mary exclaimed, "My soul glorifies the Lord" (Luke 1:46). Again, the King James translates it, "doth magnify." Mary knew her praise would draw the attention of her hearers (us included) to God her Savior.

Western culture is preoccupied with self. We are inundated with messages extolling the virtues of self-esteem, self-awareness, self-expression. In contrast, the Bible calls us to Christ-awareness and expressions of His divine life and character. As the Western church drinks from the well of the prevailing narcissism, it becomes increasingly incapable of the sacrificial, servant mentality intrinsic to world missions. Instead, it turns its ears to the preachers of self-realization, only to walk away empty. In this diseased Western milieu, worship, with its focus and effects, is a critical component of both prevention and cure. God uses worship—our eternal vocation—to remind us that we exist for a higher purpose than personal gratification. True poverty is not the absence of money but the lack of high purpose.

5. Our Sensitivity to God Increases

Corporate worship increases our sensitivity to the voice of the Spirit and sharpens our discernment. When David said God is "enthroned upon [inhabits] the praises of Israel" (Psalm 22:3, NASB), he was not referring to God's omnipresence. David knew about omnipresence. He asks, "Where can I go from your Spirit? / Where can I flee from your presence?" (Psalm 139:7). Instead, David is referring to God's manifested presence. When God manifests His presence through the activity of the Spirit, His people learn to recognize His voice and His working. They have their senses trained through practice, enabling them to test prophetic utterances. They are able to test all things and hold fast to that which is good. Certainly this is preferable to the two options widely practiced in the Western church: an undiscerning gullibility that holds fast to seemingly anything, and an equally deficient traditionalism. Some seem prepared to embrace almost any wind of doctrine. Others are quick to doubt all things and to hold fast to whatever is familiar.

6. Our Enemy Is Hindered

Since the Lord inhabits the praises of His people, worship has a hindering effect on the activity of the enemy. Often I have seen a meeting transformed as people worshiped and praised God. Not just church services. But deliverance sessions, counseling sessions, prayer meetings.

The manifestation of God that accompanies worship has a binding effect upon the activities of Satan. And you can be certain Satan is active wherever and whenever the saints are thinking seriously about missions.

7. People Are Convicted of Sin

Corporate worship produces conviction of sin. Sin has to be dealt with before missions will move forward with anointing and power. Isaiah beheld God "high and exalted" (Isaiah 6:1).

"Woe to me!" he cries. "I am ruined! For I am a man of unclean lips, and I live among a people of unclean lips, and my eyes have seen the King, the

LORD Almighty" (Isaiah 6:5). No one had preached to Isaiah about sin. He simply saw the glory of the Lord and heard the praise and worship of heaven. He was made aware of his sinfulness by the contrast with what he saw and heard. Often we attempt to convince people of sin and coerce confession from people who haven't begun to see the holiness and majesty of God. The danger of this pressure approach is that it easily produces legalism. Legalism encourages sin and consequently lends itself to the accusing activity of the devil. By contrast, the conviction of Isaiah produced a "Here am I. Send me!" response.

Much More Remains to Be Explored

These seven benefits accruing to the worshiping church are by no means all. For instance, I haven't touched on the connection between worship and the grace of giving. In a culture hypnotized by a passion for consuming, that is significant. Nor have I examined the linkage between the worship of God, who desires all people everywhere to repent, and an expanded world perspective. I have not touched on worship as it relates to sound doctrine. We live in a culture infatuated with relativism, a culture tolerant of everything but truth. I have not touched upon worship as it relates to the missionary and his or her task of evangelism. Such things are best discovered in application.

Today the Western church seeking to be missionary struggles against a potent mix. There is antiinstitutionalism and there is a virulent secularism. One militates against church structure, the other against church life. Both are against missions. For some of God's servants, laboring in places where secularization and affluence are dominant, worship may not seem to hold much promise for stirring hearts to world evangelism. But remember, the weapons of our warfare are not fleshly, but spiritual. Even those who have been influenced by the fleeting pleasures of life still are afflicted by pain. They are still troubled by the lack of meaning in life. They wrestle with the inevitability of death.

Too long we have relied on information and argument alone. It is time to recover worship as the motivation for missions. In both Old and New Testaments, worship is linked with the expansion of God's kingdom. God is seeking people who will worship Him in Spirit and in truth.

Those who take worship seriously will be best positioned and equipped to touch the lives of potential worshipers who haven't yet come home.

Missions and Prayer

CHAPTER
8

by Fred A. Hartley, III

THE NORTH AMERICAN CHURCH FACES A CRISIS. Its missionary force is imploding. Mission boards are having to downsize. They have stretched their shrinking dollars to the limit. Many people are questioning whether the vibrant overseas missionary work of the past two centuries can be sustained, let alone accelerated.

And what is behind the crisis? A sick church. The sending church is in poor health. Talk to the furloughing missionaries. They will tell you how heartbroken they are over the apathy they sense in our homeland churches. The prevailing worldliness shocks them. So does the evident surrender to materialism.

To call this problem a crisis is not an exaggeration. We are nearer than ever to the goal of winning the final tribe, the final people group. To cut back now would be an unmitigated tragedy. And although we frequently measure the malaise in terms of money, the problem is not primarily financial. Primarily it is a spiritual problem.

By and large, the North American church is spiritually anemic and backslidden. It is spiritually substandard. It lacks fire power. How can such a church continue to send out and support church-planting missionaries to other countries? How can it export a vibrant spirituality that it does not possess? Virtually every evangelical ministry in North America feels this same sense of frustration.

Confronted by such dark prospects, we need a window of hope. We find it in a brief statement spoken by Jesus—His only prayer request in all the Scriptures. Christ's simple request is brimming over with enough vision, passion, methodology and fire power to refuel our lagging mission. It can rethrust us into a global impact such as the world has yet to see. Here it is:

> *Ask the Lord of the harvest . . . to send out workers into his harvest field.* (Matthew 9:38)

Other Voices, Other Eras

Before we look closer at these words of Jesus, let's turn back the clock almost a century. In 1900 Andrew Murray addressed the exact same crisis in his landmark book, *The Key to the Missionary Problem.* David Bryant, founder and president of Concerts of Prayer International, calls the book "the most influential . . . I've ever read." Murray terms the problem "a personal one." By that he means it is not primarily a lack of vision, methodology, obedience or even finances. Rather, the people in the sending organizations have lost their personal, intimate love relationship with Jesus. They are no longer filled with the Holy Spirit. Therefore, it is impossible for them to bear spiritual fruit in their mission for God. Even if they had unlimited money and missionaries and the best of methods, still they could not.

Murray cites the small Moravian community known as Herrnhut—"the Lord's Watch." Under the leadership of their pastor, Count Nicholas Lewis von Zinzendorf, Herrnhut experienced a Pentecost. Years later, Zinzendorf recalled the event:

> The fate of Herrnhut hung in the balance, whether it was to become a sect, or to take its place in the church of our Savior. After [my] address of three or four hours, the power of the Holy Spirit decided for the latter. The foundation principle was laid down, that we were to set aside the thought of being Reformers, and to look after ourselves. What the Savior did after that . . . cannot be expressed. The whole place was indeed a veritable dwelling of God with men; and on the thirteenth of August [1722] it passed into continual praise. I, then, quieted down and entered the Sabbath rest. (pages 53-54)

Members of the group remembered with awe the "signs and wonders." They wrote of "the whole congregation bow[ing] under the sense of God's presence." Of people "sometimes at night in the field beseeching the Savior to pardon their sins and make them His own." On August 22, 1722, they this note in the record:

> Today we considered how needful it is that our Church, which is as yet in her infancy and has in Satan such a mighty enemy, should guard herself . . . and have an unceasing, holy watch kept against him. We resolved, therefore, to light a

freewill offering of intercession, which should burn night and day.

A 100-Year Prayer Meeting

As amazing as it seems, that prayer meeting lasted "night and day," 365 days a year, for *100 years!*

The Herrnhut community quickly sent out missionary teams to Turkey, Morocco and Greenland. The community itself experienced times of continual revival. During that 100 years, they sent out 600 teams of missionaries all over the world.

Reaching for a more immediate illustration, Andrew Murray referred to his contemporary, John R. Mott. Mott had begun the Student Volunteer Movement on college campuses under the motto, "The Evangelization of the World in This Generation." Mott's vision was a prayer movement that would revive the church. Through a revived church, Christ could reach the final, unreached people of the world. Mott spoke on countless college campuses and to Christian organizations, challenging them to adopt the Herrnhut model of prayer. He asked, "What has been done at Herrnhut that is not reproducible everywhere else among us?" Mott's message did indeed revive a pioneer missionary thrust at the turn of the last century. He helped a generation rediscover Christ's only prayer request.

Armin R. Gesswein, the 20th century revival prayer pacesetter, has often reminded us: "The only thing Christ left behind when He ascended into heaven was a prayer meeting." But with what outcome!

Our Lord's Own Example

Jesus Himself set a prayer example that probably no one else has completely matched. Luke has preserved for us the record:

- Jesus began His ministry with a 40-day solo prayer meeting (with fasting) in the desert (Luke 4:1-13)
- As Jesus' public ministry picked up speed, He continued to maintain the habit of private prayer (Luke 5:16)
- Prior to calling the 12 apostles, Jesus spent an entire night in prayer (Luke 6:12-16)
- Jesus took His three key disciples, Peter, James and John, to a mountain for a prayer meeting. As Jesus was praying, He was transfigured (Luke 9:28-29)
- As He sent out the 72 to preach, Jesus urged them to pray (Luke 10:1-2)
- Jesus was concluding a personal prayer time when His disciples requested, "Teach us to pray" (Luke 11:1)
- Jesus immediately proceeded to teach them what we have come to call "The Lord's Prayer" (Luke 11:2-4) and followed it with instruction about persevering in prayer and about praying in faith (Luke 11:5-13)
- As Jesus drove the merchants from the temple court, He quoted His Father's statement: "My house will be a house of prayer" (Luke 19:45-46)
- On their last night together before His crucifixion, Jesus invited His disciples to a

protracted prayer meeting in a garden on the Mount of Olives. He exhorted them, "Pray that you will not fall into temptation" (Luke 22:39-46)

- As He hung on the cross, Jesus prayed for those who had crucified Him (Luke 23:34)

Did Jesus' example and teaching make an impression on the disciples? In his later treatise, Luke says, "They all joined together constantly in prayer, along with the women and Mary the mother of Jesus, and with his brothers" (Acts 1:14).

From all of these references, it is clear that Jesus considered prayer to be vital. For Christ, prayer was both the launching pad and lifeline of all activity. And He passed on to His followers this priority of prayer.

Encouraging Signs

Today we are seeing encouraging signs of a prayer revival. We are also seeing a most remarkable rediscovery of Christ's only prayer request. New, fresh prayer initiatives are being launched in every nation, among every age group. These are not prayer-for-prayer's-sake initiatives. These are prayer initiatives with a vision of the last nation being reached through a revived church. David Bryant, in his landmark book, *The Hope at Hand* (Baker Books, 1995), documents the following:

- In 1993, 300 leaders from 166 denominations, representing almost half the Protestant churches in North America, gathered for a national consultation on prayer

- In New York City, there are an estimated 10,000 prayer groups that meet each week
- The AD 2000 and Beyond prayer initiative has mobilized 25 million Christians praying "through the window" to reach the largest unreached group people—the Muslims
- In Seoul, Korea, 100,000 high school students gathered three days and nights for prayer and praise. And 500,000 gathered in Yoida Plaza in the center of the city to fast and pray 12 hours for revival

Those are only a few clips from a full-length film brimming with revival prayer initiatives.

The following prayer covenant has been an inspiration to many grass-roots intercessors:

A Solemn Covenant

We bow before You, Almighty God, to rend our hearts and not our garments. We come with a deep desperation over the lukewarm condition of Your church and the increased evil in our society. We repent of holding to a form of godliness but denying its power.

We believe You are calling all believers around the world to join in revival praying. We link arms for the sake of spiritual awakening and world evangelization. We are convinced it is Your will to reach the world through a revived church. Therefore:

- *We devote ourselves to Your Son, the Lord Jesus Christ, in brokenness, repentance and obedience*

- *We declare our absolute dependence on You. You are the world's only hope. And the world can only know You as Your Name and the good news of salvation through Your Son are proclaimed by a revived church*
- *We determine to pray until revival comes. Whatever the cost, we resolve in advance to pay it. Moreover, we will promote this call as broadly as possible throughout the Body of Christ*

Three weeks before his death, eminent evangelical scholar J. Edwin Orr summarized in one simple statement his 60 years' study of great spiritual awakenings around the world. He said: "Whenever God is ready to do something new with His people, He always sets them to praying."

Orr should certainly have known what he was talking about. He held two earned doctorates in his field of revival studies. Brant, who quotes Orr's statement, says he based it on the words of Matthew Henry, the renowned Bible commentator, who said years earlier, "Whenever God is ready to show great mercy to His people, He always sets them a-praying" (*The Hope at Hand,* page 247). Orr went on to comment: "I have never known of so much prayer for awakening as we are seeing at present. My only fear is that we [will] begin to be proud that we are praying so much!"

The Focus, the Fullness, the Fulfillment

As we look more closely at Christ's only prayer request, we note its *focus, fullness* and *fulfillment.*

Christ Jesus wants our *focus* to be on Him, the Lord of the harvest. He wants to restore our deep love for Him in our daily worship. Above all else, He wants us to love the Lord our God with everything we're worth. Spiritual renewal begins with a revival of our love relationship with Jesus Christ.

From that focus, we move on to *fullness*. God wants us to receive the fullness of His Holy Spirit in personal and corporate revival. In our own hearts and in our church He wants us to be filled with His Spirit. The idea of fullness is implied in the phrase, "send out" (NIV), or "thrust forth" (KJV). Where there is no fullness, there can be no thrust. This is why Jesus charged His disciples to "stay and pray" before they would "go and preach." Jesus said of Himself, "The Son can do nothing by himself; he can do only what he sees his Father doing" (John 5:19). He said to His disciples, "Freely you have received, freely give" (Matthew 10:8). It is only from the fullness we receive from Christ that we are able to have a ministry of fullness to others.

The *fulfillment* comes as Christ sends out Spirit-empowered "workers into His harvest field." Fulfillment will never come without fullness. And fullness will never come without focus. If we jump from focus to fulfillment, we are playing missionary leapfrog, and our mission will implode. There are no shortcuts. Christ's only prayer request was indeed a precise model for action. It was a pattern that has been followed time and time again throughout history. And, by God's grace and Spirit, it is about to be followed once again in a final thrust to evangelize the last tribe and tongue.

We Need Liftoff!

At Cape Canaveral there is a launching pad used

for the Space Shuttle. They know it at the Cape as Pad 39. It was built with most unusual specifications. I am told it measures 390 feet wide, 345 feet long and an incredible *48 feet in depth*. It is of steel-reinforced, poured concrete.

The Space Shuttle, if its mission is to succeed, must have a launching pad capable of withstanding the required thrust. What a picture of prayer!

If our North American missionary thrust is to be renewed, it needs a prayer base as thick as Pad 39!

"Ask the Lord of the harvest . . . to send out workers into his harvest field." It is the only prayer request Jesus left for His church. It is crystal clear. It is a request Jesus has never retracted. We need to let that request hold us radically accountable.

God knows we need ignition. God knows we need liftoff!

Missions and the Local Churches

CHAPTER

9

by Harvey A. Town

I T WAS A HOT MID-AUGUST DAY IN Montana's Mission Valley. Wheat harvest was in full swing. Just west of Polson, I was driving the last of five combines. We were cutting our way around a large wheat field on the Van Voth farm.

As the sun began to drop behind the mountain ridge to the west, the breeze died. Heavy dust from my machine hung in the still air and settled over me like a fluffy quilt. How I longed for an air-conditioned cab!

Through the harvest dust that was smothering me, I suddenly saw a red Dodge pickup stirring its own huge cloud of dust. It bounced across the stubble until it was alongside the leading combine, the one my boss was operating. The pickup driver ran to the combine ladder and climbed up beside my boss. I could tell the two men were in animated conversation, my boss several times nodding his head affirmatively. Seemingly satisfied, the truck driver jumped down from the combine ladder, hurried back to his truck and roared away.

Harvest days are long, hot and dirty. The following day, we continued to thresh and haul wheat.

About seven o'clock that evening, I saw the same red pickup charging up to my boss's combine. Another vigorous conversation. More affirmative nods. When the pickup appeared on the *third* evening, my curiosity got the best of me. Who was this persistent man in the pickup? What did he want?

I learned that his name was Harris. We were scheduled to cut his fields next. He wanted to make sure of that! When would we arrive? As soon as we finished this job. Mr. Harris came every day to make sure his fields were next on our schedule.

I remember well the day our machines pulled into the Harris farm. The tall steel bins were cleaned and ready. The machinery to auger the grain was in place. The wide barbed-wire gate into the field was open. Trucks to do the hauling were at the ready.

"Good Job!"

As we made our first cut around the quarter-mile field, we checked our wind and our screens to be sure we were not throwing kernels with the chaff. I was still driving last. As I turned at the far end of the field, I noticed that back near the gate there was a dark form in the stubble moving slowly along where the chaff had fallen from my machine. As I came up the backside of the field approaching the gate, I could see that it was Mr. Harris. He was down on all fours, crawling along in the stubble, occasionally blowing away the chaff to see how many kernels of wheat were scattered on the ground. As my combine came alongside him, Mr. Harris climbed up my ladder. Putting his mouth near my ear so I could hear him above the roar of my machine, he yelled, "Good job!"

I learned some things that day that I have never forgotten: There is an urgency in gathering the harvest. And in the heart of the owner there is a deep passion that the harvest not be wasted. Every kernel is important.

Those lessons of urgency and passion come through in Jesus' parable of the workers in the vineyard (Matthew 20:1-16). Just in case we would miss the meaning, Jesus says, "The kingdom of heaven is like—" and then He tells the parable. The disciples certainly caught Jesus' sense of urgency and His own passion as they saw firsthand His deep feelings for people. Jesus saw the harvest ripe and ready for reaping, but only a few harvesters.

On a different occasion in another place, Jesus was tired, thirsty and hungry. He sat by the well outside Sychar in Samaria to rest and wait for the disciples to return with lunch. You know the story in John 4. Jesus saw a woman's need and offered her living water. At that moment the disciples arrived with food. The woman rushed away to tell her village friends about Jesus. "Could this be the Christ?" she asked excitedly (4:29). Back at the well, the disciples were pressing Jesus to eat.

Jesus answered, "I have food to eat that you known nothing about. . . . My food . . . is to do the will of him who sent me and to finish his work" (4:34). The disciples supposed someone had brought Him food while they were shopping. Meanwhile, the villagers, their curiosity aroused by the woman's testimony, headed out to meet Jesus for themselves. Jesus, seeing them, said to His disciples, "Open your eyes and look at the fields! They are ripe for harvest" (4:35).

Urgency. Passion. Commitment. In watching

Jesus and listening to Him, the disciples sensed His consuming desire to do God's will and save lost people. Is it any wonder that "many believed"?

Missionaries in Kobe, Japan

For several years, my wife Joyce and I lived and ministered in Kobe, Japan. We cared for missionaries' children and did some church planting. Both of us were involved in evangelism through English conversation classes, using the Bible as our textbook. To enlist students, I ran an ad in the English language newspaper announcing the time and place of my class.

Two sisters who had grown up in Singapore but had recently moved to Kobe were among those who came. Both Hiong and Siong were in their early twenties. They already had a good grasp of English, and I found them to be quick learners. One evening after class I asked them if they were Christians. My question seemed to puzzle them, so I explained what a Christian is.

"Oh," they responded, "then we are Christians!" Later I learned their story.

A Christian businessman from America was in Singapore. In his business contacts he met a young Singaporian—the older brother of these two women—and gave him an English Bible. The young man read the Bible and became a believer. He longed to see his family members also come to Christ. So he bought an English Bible and sent it to his two sisters in Kobe. With it he wrote a letter explaining how he had become a Christian. Hiong and Siong were touched by his letter and began to read the Bible. Soon they too committed their lives to the

Savior, Jesus Christ. It was just shortly thereafter that they read my ad in the newspaper and joined the class.

"Yes, we are Christians," they said.

I've often thought about that anonymous Christian businessman. He was simply a member of some local church back in the States. But he took seriously Christ's commission: "As you are going [that's the literal meaning of Jesus' words], make disciples." Pursuing a demanding schedule, possibly fighting jet lag, amid a strange culture, he nevertheless was seeking the harvest. Did he just happen to have an extra Bible? I suspect he planned it that way. He was looking for someone spiritually hungry. Because he was prepared and prayerful, the Holy Spirit gave him opportunity to participate in the harvest.

That's exciting! People going into their busy work days prepared. People prayerfully anticipating that they will gather some grain in the process of doing their business. Their numbers are many. Their sense of urgency and passion are an inspiration to those who join them in the harvest.

Hospitality and the Harvest

In our forty years of marriage and ministry, Joyce and I have had many people in our home. Often we receive notes from these who joined our family circle for a meal or an evening. Invariably there are kind words of thanks and perhaps a reminder of a shared memory.

Living in Japan's port city of Kobe gave us many opportunities for this kind of hospitality. Kobe has a natural deep sea harbor. United States Navy ships would often call there—carriers, destroyers, submarines. At Kobe Union Church a group of us made a practice of inviting sailors to our homes for food and fun. The men liked to play with the children. We would hear them say, "I've got a kid sister just like you!" or "I have a boy just about your age!

One of the fellows who visited us was involved in shore patrol. His responsibility was to see that his buddies didn't get into trouble while they were ashore. His last name was Beaver. When it came to witnessing for Christ, he was Eager Beaver! The day after one of his visits with us he was on duty, but that evening he telephoned. I could hear the traffic and the city noises in the background as I listened to his animated voice. He had been working all day with the man who headed the foreign section of the Kobe Police Department. After sharing the gospel with this Japanese, he had led the man to Christ! Could I do some follow-up? Would there be room for the man in my English Bible class?

This high-up official was not Beaver's only trophy that day. He told me he had also led a restaurant waitress to the Lord!

The police official began to attend my Bible study class. He was there faithfully every week. And Beaver sailed off. We never saw him again. But sharing Christ in a foreign port as he went about his duties was a way of life for him.

I know a lot of "Beavers"! You probably know some, too. Committed Christians, members of local churches, who in the course of their daily routine are gathering the harvest. Maybe you are one of them! The Scriptures say: "Those who are wise will shine like the brightness of the heavens, and those who lead many to righteousness, like the stars for ever and ever" (Daniel 12:3).

You Are a Part of God's Missionary Plan

God has only one plan for gathering the harvest. Jesus stated it well when He said, "The Son of Man came to seek and to save what was lost" (Luke 19:10) and again, "As the Father has sent me, I am sending you" (John 20:21). "Go and make disciples of all nations" (Matthew 28:19) were among the last words Jesus spoke to His followers. Today every Christian has the privilege of participating in the harvest. Never in the history of the human race have more people been investing time, talent and treasure in God's kingdom work.

As a teenager, a statement by Jesus gripped my heart: "Whoever wants to save his life will lose it, but whoever loses his life for me will find it" (Matthew 16:25). At age 17 I offered my life to the Savior. Since that day I have endeavored to be a good steward of all the resources the Lord has entrusted to me. He has given me 24 hours a day. He has given me spiritual gifts and natural talents. He has put under my care material resources. I have sought to use all of this in the harvest. I don't want to be embarrassed when I account to Jesus for my spiritual journey here on earth.

But it is more than the day of reckoning that motivates me. I'm eager to complete the harvest and thus hasten Christ's return to earth (see 2 Peter 3:11-12). After 40 years of missionary and pastoral ministry, I am more excited than ever about the decision I made when I was still in high school. Following and serving Jesus have enriched my life far more than I ever anticipated. I feel wealthy!

It was missionary Jim Elliot who said, "He is no

fool who gives what he cannot keep to gain what he cannot lose." When Peter, speaking for the disciples, reminded Jesus of all they had forsaken (as if Jesus needed the reminder!), He replied: "Everyone who has left houses or brothers or sisters or father or mother or children or fields for my sake will receive a hundred times as much and will inherit eternal life" (Matthew 19:29). Even those who make their commitment later in life will receive ample reward. Our Master is most generous in rewarding our service, as His parable of the workers in the vineyard indicates (Matthew 20:1-16). If you haven't yet found your place in the harvest, it's not too late. Start today!

On an Air Canada flight from Calgary to Regina I was reading the airline's magazine. I came upon this statement in an article by Richard Field and David Van Seters: "All constructive plans, actions and accomplishments are fueled by expectations. The most vital key in management, therefore, is to develop high expectations."

The Lord Jesus declared: "This gospel of the kingdom will be preached in the whole world as a testimony to all nations, and then the end will come" (Matthew 24:14). His statement got His disciples' attention. Talk about high expectations! Jesus is coming as soon as the harvest is gathered! Is it any wonder that so many local churches give evangelism and missions high priority? If you are a Christian, you are a member of the harvest crew. Your efforts in prayer, in giving and in loving your neighbors are a very signficant part in gathering the spiritual grain. Jesus will say "Well done!" to you. And while you're busy for Him down here, He's busy preparing a place for you up there (see John 14:2-3). What wonderful expectations we enjoy!

Is the Holy Spirit in Control of Your Life?

Are you possibly reading this with a deep-down uneasy feeling about your lost opportunities? Or maybe you're thinking, "I've tried to witness and failed" or "I tried, and things just didn't go the way I had expected."

Try again! Begin all over. Don't give up! Perhaps your disappointment came because you were not depending on the Holy Spirit. Perhaps you failed to pray. Have you asked God to give you love for your neighbor? We must depend on God. He empowers us as we give Him our bodies and our wills to use as He chooses. He brings us into a relationship with Himself that allows His work to be accomplished in and through us. Sometimes we are not even conscious of the work that is taking place as we go about our daily activities. As we present ourselves for His service, we may be joyously surprised by the outcome!

During college I worked summers at Glacier National Park. One summer a high school classmate and I were living in a tent, "batching it" to save more money for our next school year. Before eating, I would always bow my head and pray. One day Jim suggested, "Why don't you teach me to do that?" The Lord had used my life to influence Jim. Later that summer he prayed to receive Christ.

I find that allowing the Holy Spirit to be in control of my life is a prerequisite to effective harvesting.

Are You Praying? Are You Accountable?

Besides making sure God is in charge, taking ample time to pray is like giving full throttle to a combine engine. When prayer is a meaningful part of my day, there is plenty of power.

It was Martin Luther who said, "If I should neglect prayer but a single day, I should lose a great deal of the fire of faith." In Acts we see the same cause-and-effect relation. The church was praying all the time! Paul said to the church in Philippi: "In everything, by prayer and petition, with thanksgiving, present your requests to God" (Philippians 4:6).

Third, do you know what helps me stay on course? Accountability. Declaring my intentions publicly so that people hold me to my purposes. It's a bit like when the Lord said, "What do you want me to do for you?" and the blind man responded, "Rabbi, I want to see" (Mark 10:51). It became a matter of public record.

For years I've written down in my appointment book the things I want to do over the course of the year. That helps me to be accountable, even if I don't mention those commitments publicly. Having someone ask me how long it has been since I've shared a clear presentation of the gospel with another person is an excellent incentive to keep my focus on the harvest!

Be a Part of the Action in Your Church

Fourth, let your pastor know that you want a part in the action at church. Be a member of the missions committee. Help decorate the church for missions conference. If you are artistic, volunteer to do the missions bulletin board. There are dozens of ways you can serve. Everybody's baby is nobody's baby. So often we think someone else will do it and so often nobody does it. As a result, nothing is done. Become an encourager of your pastor and your church's missionaries by sending upbeat notes or letters to them. Read the many exciting missionary story books to your children or to neighborhood kids. These accounts will stimulate their minds and hearts toward the harvest. Send a care package to a student preparing to become a harvester. Pray that the Lord will guide you in your own service for Him.

If you examine Jesus' Great Commission carefully, you'll see that He made room for everyone to be involved. The Commission wasn't just to the remaining 11 disciples. Do you see the clause ". . . but some doubted" (Matthew 28:17)? By that point there were no doubters among Jesus' remaining 11 disciples. So this had to be a larger company, perhaps the "more than five hundred" (1 Corinthians 15:6) that Paul speaks of.

Moreover, the emphasis is not on the "go" but on the "make disciples." Making disciples is the imperative. As I suggested earlier, it could well be translated, "As you go, make disciples." As you go to work, as you go to the market, as you go on a business trip to Manila or Montevideo, *make disciples*.

Jesus expects you to be involved in the harvest. There is a place for you. Find that place. Do something.

How Much Does It Cost?

May I introduce you to Ray and Sheila? Ray and Shiela were a young couple in one of the local churches my wife and I served. The congregation was preparing to relocate to new property and new facilities. Members were making unusual commitments of their resources so this relocation could take place.

As Ray and Sheila prayed about their participation, they felt they should give all of their savings to the project. They had been putting money aside to buy their first home. Without that substantial down payment, they could not qualify for a mortgage. Their dream of buying a home would be put off. Nevertheless, Ray and Sheila obeyed what they believed to be God's prompting. They gave the whole amount.

I remember the night they told the congregation what the Lord had asked them to do. People at first sat in stunned silence and then burst into joyous applause.

(I was also around a few months later when God honored Ray and Sheila's obedience. He provided them with a more advantageous mortgage. They were able to buy—at once—a better home than they had planned to get.)

How much does it cost to prepare the soil, plant the seed and thresh the grain? Plenty! So also with the spiritual harvest. It takes the resources of many faithful people with a joyful generosity that goes far beyond 10 percent giving. I hope you have already made the discovery of munificent, joyful giving. The Lord in His Word encourages us wonderfully in our stewardship. "Give and it will be given to you," Jesus promises. "A good measure, pressed down, shaken together and running over, will be poured into your lap. For with the measure you use, it will be measured to you" (Luke 6:38).

I recall a time when Joyce and I made a significant financial commitment above our regular giving. In effect, it amounted to more than a double tithe over a three year period. The very week that we completed our financial commitment, we received a check in the mail equal to the total amount of our extra giving! God does not necessarily reward in kind. But He rewards. If we are faithful stewards of the resources God has entrusted to us, He will see that we don't lack.

Mr. Harris, the wheat farmer in western Montana, had a sense of urgency about his harvest. He had a passion to preserve every possible kernel. The American businessman in Singapore and my Navy friend, Beaver, had a similar attitude toward the spiritual harvest. So did Ray and Sheila, the young couple willing to postpone their own desires in favor of God's kingdom.

Gathering the spiritual harvest is the high privilege and solemn commission of every member of Christ's church. It is those members fired with a Christ-like concern and holy passion to reap the ripened harvest. It is those members praying and giving and witnessing right where they live and serve.

Have you sensed the urgency in your own spirit? Day by day, are you renewing your commitment to be a faithful harvester?

> *Come and join the reapers, all the kingdom seekers,*
> *Laying down your life to find it in the end.*
> *Come and share the harvest, help to light the darkness,*
> *For the Lord is calling faithful men.*
> (Twila Paris)

The
Fourfold
Gospel

Missions and the Saving Christ

by Steve M. Irvin

CHAPTER

10

DECLARATION OF PURPOSE. MISSION STATEMENT. Vision Manifesto. Everywhere you go these days, organizations and businesses have posted their reason for existing. Banks, restaurants, civic groups, even churches find that clarifying "the main thing" focuses their goal. It gives them identity, it helps them avoid peripheral pursuits that distract rather than contribute to their central purpose.

You can imagine the confusion three young entrepreneurs had as they opened a new restaurant. One was keen on hamburgers. Another had a penchant for Chinese food. The third loved French cuisine. Being equal partners, they finally settled on a mixed menu of all three lines. Needless to say, their business venture ended in disaster.

Now that definitive mission statements are so popular with businesses and organizations, many are advocating the same for individuals. These people believe all of us could be better focused if we had our own personalized statement of purpose.

Jesus Came for a Fundamental Purpose

If Jesus, during His sojourn on earth, had posted such a statement, how would it have read? Certainly from our study of His life and teachings we could put together such a manifesto for Him. But it is not necessary. Jesus did it for us. In His own words, He concisely states His mission on earth. In response to questions about the conversion of Zacchaeus, Jesus says, "The Son of Man came to seek and to save what was lost" (Luke 19:10).

In those few words Jesus sets forth the fundamental purpose of His coming to earth. "What was lost" describes all of humankind, separated from our Creator by rebellion and sin. In His statement we find the essential mission of the saving Christ. To be sure, we may point to other good things He did during His ministry on earth. But those other things point to the ultimate work that gives meaning to all else: He came to seek and to save what was lost.

We contemplate the simplicity of that profound statement. We try to plumb its infinite meaning within the purposes of God. It strikes home to our hearts. It fills us with gratitude. At the same time, it calls us to assess our own goals and priorities. Surely every follower of Christ should incorporate into his or her life the same dominant mission principle.

When we view world evangelization from this perspective, it suddenly assumes new meaning. It is not a spiritual hobby or an exercise in ascetic disciplines. Neither is it simply an antiquated obligation. It gets to the very core of what it means to be part of the body of Christ.

Jesus Is the Source of Missions

As we look to Him, the Author and Finisher of our salvation, we discover He is the very *Source of missions*. He is the Source because all authority in heaven and on earth has been vested in Him and He commands us to go (Matthew 28:18-20). He is also the Source because His incarnation is the fountain from which springs even the concept of going and proclaiming. He declares, "As the Father has sent me, I am sending you" (John 20:21).

Robert A. Jaffray, noted pioneer missionary to China and southeast Asia, died in a Japanese internment camp in Indonesia. At age 71, he was a victim of starvation and inhuman wartime treatment. In Jaffray's biography, *Let My People Go,* author A.W. Tozer reflects upon the death of this apostle-like figure:

> *In this picture of the saint dying of exhaustion while evil men spread themselves and, for a little hour, throw their weight around, we have in miniature the sad history of the world. Any rebellious thought we might be tempted to entertain is quickly dispelled by the knowledge that when God would save men from their moral suicide He had to be born in a manger and die on a cross. Jaffray was the willing servant of such a God as this. Under what more fitting conditions then could he die, a man who believed as he believed and loved as he loved? He would not have had it otherwise. He chose to die in the East Indies.*

This "incarnational model" becomes a reminder

to us, as Tozer noted in another work. The first task of the church is not just to proclaim Christ, but to be *worthy* to proclaim Christ. As the Savior works out His life—the Christ life—in us, our lives become our most effective mode of communication. For missions must reach out to the whole world, beginning with our own sphere of influence.

It was precisely in reference to people like Zacchaeus, the Jewish tax collector, that Jesus was called the friend of sinners (see Matthew 11:19). Yet we find ourselves repulsed by increased immorality and even sacrilege in our decadent society. Our tendency is to put up barriers to the world. We want to escape to refuges of our own making. We wish to distance ourselves as much as possible from contact with sinners.

We Need to See the World as Jesus Saw it

The Lord Jesus Christ, the Source of our life and mission, bids us open our hearts to see the world as He sees it. He asks us to love sinful people with His love and to win them to Himself. After all, if the saving Christ lives within us, how can we not help but seek for others to know Him as Savior, too?

Among the Paez Indian tribe of Colombia, the name of Porfirio Ocaña will long be remembered. He was the patriarch of the church of the Lord Jesus Christ founded among this people group some 50 years ago. Recently he died, and the testimony of his faithfulness to his Lord stirs the hearts of all who hear it.

As the first convert from among the Paez, Porfirio faced intense persecution. And when he began to preach openly of Christ the Savior, the spiritual opposition was merciless. He was actually tortured for his faith. Yet he persevered, seeking every opportunity to share the gospel with fellow tribespeople and win them to the Lord. He sowed in tears, but there has been a harvest of joy. Today hundreds, possibly thousands, have come to know Christ.

Jesus Is the Scope of Missions

But we dare not limit our focus to those physically and culturally near us. We must see the Lord Jesus as also defining *the scope of missions*. The Son of God did not come to touch only those living in Palestine. He came as "the Savior of the world" (1 John 4:14).

Before Jesus' conception, the angel Gabriel had already announced to Zechariah the birth of John the Baptist, Jesus' forerunner. He would "make ready a people prepared for the Lord" (Luke 1:17). True to prediction, John did exactly that. Luke sums up his ministry in the words of the prophet Isaiah:

> *A voice of one calling in the desert,*
> *"Prepare the way for the Lord,*
> *make straight paths for him."* (Luke 3:4)

Luke concludes with the words, "And all mankind will see God's salvation" (3:6). *All mankind.* John himself, upon seeing Jesus, exclaimed to those within hearing: "Look, the Lamb of God, who takes away the sin of the world!" (John 1:29). *The world.* The scope of our missionary efforts goes beyond family and community to all nations. It looks to proclaim Christ the Savior to every possible person.

We Live in Isolation

We live in ever-increasing isolation. Naively we thought that the crumbling of the Berlin Wall and the tearing asunder of the Iron Curtain would ease conflict. To our sad bewilderment, ethnic conflicts continue to tear apart whole countries. They are leading to the wholesale slaughter of human life, whether in Eastern Europe or Black Africa. The Kurds find no home in Central Asia. The Palestinians thought they had a home, but extremists on both sides of this perennial issue will not allow peace. European "skin heads" burn to death immigrants of darker skin. Louis Farrakhan perceives an irremediable attitude of white supremacy in America. He calls for a separate homeland for African-Americans.

In this morass of racial prejudice, nationalistic fervor and ethnic cleansings, we in the church are at risk. Not always has the church been immune from spiritual "Balkanization." The current tendencies toward isolationism and protectionism can seep into the body of Christ. The slogan "America First!" may have its defenders in the economic and political realms. But such an attitude in the kingdom of God is indefensible. Christ "is the atoning sacrifice for our sins, and not only for ours but also for the sins of the whole world." (1 John 2:2). He came to earth because "God . . . loved the world" (John 3:16). The angel announced to the shepherds, "I bring you good news of great joy that will be for all the people" (Luke 2:10). The scope of missions will always include people from every nation, for the Lord will not return until this gospel has been "preached in the whole world as a testimony to all nations" (Matthew 24:14).

Jesus Is the Soul of Missions

Finally, the saving Christ is *the soul of missions*. He is at the heart of the message we share. On Him we must continually fix our eyes. The bottom line is not a commodity or a blessing. He is a Person. We must continue to return to the Soul Himself. We must proclaim Christ, and Him alone, as the fully sufficient Savior and Lord.

This may seem too rudimentary to merit emphasis. It is "obvious" that the saving Christ is our message. Yet to hear the pure and simple gospel of Jesus—His life, death, resurrection and ascension (1 Corinthians 15:3-5)—is rare. Our tendency is to embellish the message. We expect, thereby, to make it more palatable to our hearers. The life of this rejected Rabbi seems too mystical for some. For others, His death is a travesty of justice that a loving Father should not have permitted. Still others refuse to believe His physical resurrection. Some think the ascension into heaven only separates "the Man of Sorrows" from the reality of our troubled world. Surely faith and repentance on the basis of so simple a message cannot be. Surely today's penetrating, logical minds deserve something more profound.

What humility it takes to come to Christ! But what faith and humility to proclaim Christ alone as the way of salvation! In our proclamation we are always struggling to maintain a balance between transcendence and relevance. If we are too sublime, our message does not get home in a practical way to our hearers. And if we try to be too relevant, we reduce the gospel to a self-improvement seminar. We blunt the cutting edge of the message people so desperately need to hear.

In my experience, I have found that people want to hear from God, not just from me. When I lift Christ up, He draws people to Himself (John 12:32).

Of course our message must be understandable and applicable to those whom we are trying to reach. But it must be the *true message*. It must be Christ! There is nothing more timely than eternity and nothing more relevant than the living Lord of creation.

Jesus Remains Our Message

Today in the body of Christ there is an emphasis on power. This concern with power and authority is deserving of attention. It is based on the biblical truth of Christ's victory over Satan and our position with Him in the heavenly realms. But we must not preach power for power's sake. Such an unhealthy emphasis strangely mirrors the world's own priorities of dominance and independence. Signs and wonders *accompany* the preaching of the gospel, but they do not replace its content.

The real power is seen in the preaching of Christ Himself. After all, the gospel is "the power of God for the salvation of everyone who believes" (Romans 1:16). Only the power of God can cleanse from sin and change a life so that it is an instrument of God's own holiness.

Other themes capture the human imagination. There are radio and television sermons on how to achieve an ecstatic spiritual experience. There are books of sermons on how to have a better marriage. There are tape series on how to be prosperous. Although these teachings may have truth in them, they cannot save. They must never become the chief concentration of our proclamation.

Paul said, "Jews demand miraculous signs and Greeks look for wisdom, but we preach Christ crucified: a stumbling block to Jews and foolishness to Gentiles, but to those whom God has called, both Jews and Greeks, Christ the power of God and the wisdom of God" (1 Corinthians 1:22-24).

As we respond in faith to the saving Christ, we become witnesses to these truths. As we yield our lives to the Lordship of Christ, He who saved us now calls us to the work that was His priority: seeking and saving the lost. Thankfully, we need not work alone. Christ is still active. Though He reigns from His throne, exalted at the right hand of the Father, He continues to minister through His Spirit.

Jesus Is the Same

Jesus continues to do what He first came to do: "to seek and to save what was lost." His work on the cross is complete, done once for all. Now He lives in us, the saving Christ, the Source, the Scope and the Soul of missions. He it is who carries out His purposes in us, His body.

Some day, around God's throne, there will be a multitude too numerous to count "from every nation, tribe, people and language" (Revelation 7:9). They will be wearing white robes, and in their hands they will hold palm branches. And they will cry out in praise:

Salvation belongs to our God,
who sits on the throne,
and to the Lamb. (Revelation 7:10)

Glory to Christ our Savior!

Missions and the Sanctifying Christ

<table>
<tr><td>

_____

CHAPTER

_____

11

_____

</td></tr>
</table>

by Keith M. Bailey

BEFORE THE TURN OF THE LAST CENTURY, a young Presbyterian missionary candidate was preparing to board an ocean liner that would take him to India. As he stepped toward the gangplank, a long-time friend of the family greeted him, handing him an envelope.

"John," she said, "wait until you are out to sea before you read this letter." John thanked the woman for coming to see him off and slipped the letter into his pocket.

It was an exciting day. As John mounted the gangplank, it was with a sense of confidence bordering on smugness. At last he was on his way to begin his life as a missionary.

Once in his cabin, he set to work unpacking his bags. The ship was leaving port when he remembered the letter in his pocket. As he read its contents, it was not at all what he had expected. His friend exhorted him to seek the Lord earnestly for the empowering of the Holy Spirit. As he read, John grew angry. He wadded up the letter and tossed it across the room.

Didn't this woman know that he had finished his academic work with high marks? He had survived the rigors of a written and oral examination before the presbytery. By all standards he was well prepared for the ministry he was setting out for. He went up on deck, hoping to forget the letter.

After several rounds of the deck, John returned to his cabin, ashamed that he had reacted so negatively to the letter. Retrieving the paper, he smoothed out the wrinkles and sat down to read its contents again. As the Holy Spirit began to deal with him, hot tears streamed down his face. Kneeling at his bunk, he asked God to cleanse his heart and endue him with the power of the Holy Spirit. In fact, during the long days of the sea voyage, he spent many hours in earnest prayer, waiting upon God.

John Hyde—for that was his name—arrived in India a much different young man than the one who had boarded the ship a few weeks earlier. And in the years that followed, he became a missionary legend. Most people now know him as Praying Hyde, the humble, godly missionary whose labors for Christ left such an impact on India.

John's elderly friend knew something about world missions that everyone else had failed to tell him. Taking the gospel of Christ to a lost world requires a clean, Spirit-filled person. John Hyde's experience is a reminder that holiness is always a factor in reaching the world. The missionary movement was launched at Pentecost with purifying tongues of fire. World evangelization is a holy and supernatural operation.

A Walk with the Holy One

The Great Commission given by Christ (Matthew

28:19-20) implies the place of holiness in carrying out this wonderful plan. Jesus said:

> *Go and make disciples of all nations, baptizing them in the name of the Father and of the Son and of the Holy Spirit, and teaching them to obey everything I have commanded you.*

Then He adds:

> *And surely I am with you always, to the very end of the age.*

Jesus assured those He sent to preach that His presence would be with them. To walk with the Savior in this work is a high expression of sanctification. The success of the missionary endeavor is found in a shared walk with the Holy One. Walking with Christ and being indwelt by Christ describes a state of inner sanctification.

Jesus' words do not mean that those who answer the call to preach Christ to the nations are sanctified by that act. It rather means that only those transformed by Christ and inhabited by Him are ready to take the gospel to the unreached. A sanctified heart is the basic requirement for missionary service. It is unthinkable that one who is impure, unconsecrated and not filled with the Spirit could serve as the ambassador of Christ to the lost.

Sanctified and Sent

World missions is not a task we take upon ourselves. It is a task we are sent to do. The Scriptures are not silent on this matter. The idea of God sending people to carry His message is first found in the Old Testament. The prophet Jeremiah tells how God sent him to preach to Judah:

The word of the LORD came to me saying,

"Before I formed you in the womb I knew you,
before you were born I set you apart;
I appointed you as a prophet to the nations."
(Jeremiah 1:4-5)

Jeremiah was overwhelmed by such a commission from God. He protested, citing his immaturity. God responded:

Do not say, "I am only a child." You must go to everyone I send you to and say whatever I command you. Do not be afraid of them, for I am with you and will rescue you. (1:7-8)

God sanctified Jeremiah before he was born. He was set apart for God as a prophet while still in his mother's womb. It was this sanctifying grace that sustained the prophet through a long and difficult ministry. The principle in both the Old and New Testaments is that God sanctifies those He sends as His spokesmen.

The testimony of Isaiah gives further confirmation to this principle. Isaiah went to the temple for spiritual solace after the death of King Uzziah, his friend. He knew the death of the king would drastically change his circumstances. It seemed that his world was falling apart. He needed some answers from God.

While he waited in the temple, the Lord made Himself visible to Isaiah. He saw God high and lifted up. The very air was charged with a sense of the Lord's holiness. Special angels were engaged in worship that was directed toward the holiness of God. The temple was ringing with the joyous cries of the seraphs, saying "Holy, holy, holy is the LORD Almighty; / the whole earth is full of his glory" (Isaiah 6:3).

Isaiah Saw His Sinfulness

For the prophet, the immediate effect of this experience was an overwhelming awareness of his own sinfulness. He cried to God in anguish of soul. A seraph flew to the altar and brought a live coal in his hand with which he touched Isaiah's lips. The angel assured the prophet that he had been cleansed. Immediately God spoke.

"Whom shall I send?" God asked. "And who will go for us?"

Without hesitation Isaiah answered, "Here am I. Send me!"

From Isaiah's experience we can learn that dedication is not enough for the person God sends. There must be the sanctifying work that cleanses the heart. The sent one must not only be surrendered fully. He must also be pure through the sanctifying effect of Christ's atonement. Such a level of holiness is both internal and outward. It is openly expressed in a person's daily walk.

The magnitude of the commission calls for a reflection of Christ in those who carry it out. Compromise will not do. The missionary who takes the gospel, the believer who stays at home and prays and those who give financially must equally demonstrate the indwelling of Christ, our Sanctifier.

The glorious and holy enterprise of world missions needs a work force that is sanctified and made ready for every good work.

On the surface, the life of a missionary may appear to be exciting and romantic. Those who have gone to the world's harvest fields know better. Being a missionary is sometimes humiliating. Only the Spirit of Christ can bring victory in that circumstance. There are times when the situation the missionary enters is frightening. It requires spiritual maturity to find the Rock who hides and protects. Missionary work can challenge a person's every resource.

Again, the work can be incredibly monotonous and dull. And what about the loneliness that sometimes brings a person to the brink of despair? Family life often becomes stressful. Relationships with fellow workers can get out of hand. Add the roars of Satan and his nagging demons that can make life a nightmare. The list would be incomplete were we not to recognize that the missionary may face a financial crunch.

Nothing in the missionary's professional training can fully prepare him or her for the realities of field life. Only a pure, Spirit-filled Christian can expect to cope. The secret is death to self and the abiding presence of the living Christ. This kind of sanctification is more than a theological concept. It is a real and personal union with Christ, the Sanctifier.

Christ, Our Pattern

The best example of a sanctified, sent servant is Christ Himself. John records an occasion when Jesus was explaining to the Jews the heavenly nature of His work. He told them that His ministry originated with the Father. The Jews were indignant that Jesus claimed God as His Father. They accused Him of blasphemy. Jesus responded:

> If he called them gods to whom the word of God came (and the Scripture cannot be broken), do you say of Him whom the Father sanctified and sent into the world, "You are blaspheming" because I said I am the Son of God?
>
> If I do not the works of My Father, do not believe Me; but if I do, though you do not believe Me, believe the works that you may know and believe that the Father is in Me and I in Him. (John 10:35-38, NKJV)

From that passage we can gather that Christ was indeed consecrated by a higher level than any Old Testament prophet or priest. The spiritual leaders of the Old Testament were consecrated by men like themselves. Christ was consecrated by the Father in heaven. Christ was also sent into the world by His Father. The sanctifying and sending of Christ was to be the model for the gospel age, the time of worldwide evangelization.

Later in his Gospel, John preserved the prayer Jesus prayed the night before His crucifixion. Jesus said to God His Father:

> My prayer is not that you take them out of the world but that you protect them from the evil one. They are not of the world, even as I am not of it. Sanctify them by the truth; your word is truth. As you sent me into the world, I have sent them into the world. For them I sanctify myself, that they too may be truly sanctified. (John 17:15-19)

Christ was praying for His disciples and for the church that would form as a result of His disciples' ministries. From the words of that prayer it is evident that we who serve Christ today as sent ones are to follow His pattern. Just as Christ was sanctified and sent into the world, so the contemporary missionary.

Jesus understands what the world is like. He knows it is a fallen, depraved system. Our planet is populated with lost people separated from God, dominated by the devil and immersed in spiritual darkness. Jesus knew that the church, like Himself, would be confronting this present evil world. Only those spiritually equipped would be able to carry out the mission of evangelizing the world.

In Two Millennia the Pattern Is Unchanged

In every age of the church, the pattern is the same. God sanctifies those He sends to preach His gospel. Christ's supreme mission in the world was His death on the cross and His resurrection from the dead. He was sanctified by the Father for that work. All the eternal purposes of God in Christ hinged on the outcome of those events. Those whom He sends to tell the nations of His triumph at the cross and tomb must be sanctified.

The words of Christ's prayer suggest three aspect of sanctification necessary for His sent ones. There must be a *renunciation* of the world. There must be a total *dedication* to Christ. There must be an *internal cleansing* by the Word of truth.

Personal holiness is necessary for those sent to present to the world the character of God. Verbal testimony alone is not enough. The Christian missionary must manifest the pure character of Christ in his or her daily walk. In this light, it is time for a renewal of biblical holiness in the whole church.

The atonement of Christ omits no human situation. The good news about Christ is "the power of God for the salvation of everyone who believes" (Romans 1:16). It announces both justification and sanctification. "The whole gospel for the whole world" is not an outdated cliché; it is a theological truth. Those who proclaim the whole gospel to the nations must themselves be made whole by the sanctifying Christ.

The interest and compassion of a missionary is on a much higher level than human altruism. His or her heart is moved by the compassion of Christ. The missionary's mind has been enlightened by God's Word on the true nature of people's plight. He or she understands that the underlying cause of people's miseries is their lostness. The Spirit-filled man or woman feels with Christ deep anguish for the unsaved, who face judgement and eternal hell. The same Sanctifier who purges the sent one's heart from sin fills that heart with the love of Christ. Christ's love impels him or her to do everything possible to bring the lost to Christ. It is this grace of sanctification that motivates the church to evangelize the world.

The Church's Missions Rests on Pentecost

It is evident from the Scriptures that the Lord of the harvest requires holiness in the lives of the harvesters. The entire missionary enterprise rests on the reality of Pentecost. Power from on high is the credential needed to effectively witness to the death and resurrection of Christ. The fire of Pentecost not only empowers but it cleanses. It fits the missionary for the Master's use.

As the missionary needs the Sanctifier, so does the church. Missions is a holy church sending out holy missionaries to do a holy work backed by holy pray-ers and holy stewards.

Methods change. The world situation changes. Educational demands intensify. But the primary qualification of the present-day missionary is still a definite and personal union with Christ, our Sanctifier.

Missions and the Healing Christ

CHAPTER

12

by Donald O. Young

W HO SAYS HEALING IS NOT FOR TODAY? Not the thousands upon thousands who take God at His Word and experience the healing touch of Jesus! Not missionaries around the world who witness the healing power of Jesus, some of them almost on a daily basis.

In the days of His ministry on earth, Jesus "appointed seventy-two," sending them out "to every town and place where he was about to go" (Luke 10:1). They went in the power and authority of His name. Jesus instructed them: "Heal the sick who are there and tell them, 'The kingdom of God is near you' " (10:9).

When they returned at the conclusion of their itinerary, they exclaimed to Jesus, "Lord, even the demons submit to us in your name" (10:17). That was a powerful declaration! These 72 "missionaries" found out through practical experience that the name of Jesus is all-powerful.

But it is Jesus' response that I find especially revealing. He said, "I saw Satan fall like lightning from heaven" (10:18). That is an awesome statement. I find it exhilarating. In essence Jesus was confirming to them, "You are right! In My name you can cast out demons. Their hold on the territories where I sent you was broken. Why? Because I gave you authority to tread upon those satanic forces. You took that authority, and I responded to your faith."

A Powerful Strategy for Missions

What a powerful strategy for missions! Think of it: Jesus our Healer, supernaturally intervening to tread down satanic forces in all nations. Let me tell you about two dramatic illustrations of this that I personally witnessed.

The first was in Côte d'Ivoire, West Africa, during the late 1970s. Traditionally Côte d'Ivoire has been largely animistic in belief, although the nation has a high percentage of Christians, both Roman Catholic and Protestant. In recent years, Islam has taken on new energy and power.

In the late 1970s, my wife and I were completing Baoulé language study. Our assignment would be to work among high school and college students in the city of Bouaké. Some 200 miles away, in the port city of Abidjan, a French evangelist, Pastor Jacques Girot, was preaching to several hundred Christians and visitors gathered for the dedication of a new church building.

During Pastor Girot's message, which centered on the power and authority in the name of Jesus, many of those in the audience began to shake uncontrollably and fall to the ground. Immediately, the African pastors present prayed over those on the ground. There was a great deliverance from demonic spirits.

The meetings continued night after night. People returned with friends and family from nearby villages to meet God. As demons were cast out of many, miraculous healings took place. Girot's message never changed. He would use a different Bible text each night, but the message was the same: "There is power, hope and healing in the name of the Lord."

An Expanded Ministry

It was not long before the church and its surrounding property became too small for the thousands of people who were coming to hear and to be healed. The church got permission to move the meetings to the soccer stadium. Crowds of up to 30,000 each night came to hear God's Word and be freed from the bondage of Satan. They came on stretchers and in wheelchairs. Crippled men and women came walking with their old wooden canes. The blind and deaf came. The paralyzed and the nearly dead came. In every case where demons were involved, these people were healed as the demons were cast out. The healings moved through every strata of society: the rich and poor, the educated and uneducated, the young and old. It reached the highest echelons of government. Even some long-time members of the President's cabinet were healed of terrible diseases. Every tribe and ethnic group were represented. No one was left out. God met everyone who came for deliverance.

As I said earlier, the Ivorien culture is largely animistic. The people believe God is good and Satan is evil. God, being good, will not harm them. Satan, being evil, will. They supposed that by dedicating their children to Satan as babies, they would be protected from his evil ways.

In reality, we were witnessing in the Jacques Girot meetings an old-fashioned power encounter. It was a contest between the powers of darkness and the powers of light. Night after night we saw the awesome power of God bringing deliverance and healing and spiritual life through the name of Jesus Christ our Lord.

A Nationwide Opportunity

For over a month the meetings continued in Abidjan. Then in an unprecedented move, the President of Côte d'Ivoire, the late Felix Houphouet-Boigny, called the evangelistic team to his office. President Boigny, himself a medical doctor, said in summary to the team members: "I don't understand what's happening, but it's good. I want my people to be healed. Take this message to every major city in Côte d'Ivoire, and I will pay the bill!"

That is how the Girot team arrived in Bouaké for ten days of meetings, three services each day. During that period I witnessed literally thousands of healings. I saw and experienced firsthand the authority given and taken in the name of the Lord Jesus Christ. It was a power encounter, not a revival. It happened largely among the pagans. These pagans were delivered, consequently healed and ultimately saved. Thousands of them became part of the body of Christ.

Since those powerful days of healing and deliverance in Côte d'Ivoire, the church has never been the same. In less than two years, attendance quadrupled. And subsequently the church has continued to grow at an amazing pace. Pastors and missionaries began preaching with new power and with powerful results. Dramatic healings continued to take place.

I can hear Jesus saying again what He said to the 72 preachers whom He sent out: "I saw Satan fall like lightning from heaven." What a powerful God we serve! What a mighty name He has! What awesome authority He has given to His church!

In South America, Too

Nearly 20 years later, in another context and on another continent, God allowed me again to see His power unleashed. The occasion began as a businessmen's conference to be held in Concepción, Chile, some six hours south of Santiago. George Woerner, a North American businessman, and I were invited to attend and speak.

The conference began Friday morning. George gave a tremendous testimony of how God had blessed his business. He used God's promise in Jeremiah 29:11-14 ("I know the plans I have for you, . . . plans to prosper you and not to harm you . . ."). In an hour's time he highlighted how his company in 20 years went from bankruptcy to prosperity.

God poured out His blessing upon the sessions. Men and women involved in all walks of business and professional life were convicted of their need to trust the Lord.

Friday and Saturday evenings, the conference joined several hundred local church people for praise and worship in a local church. On Friday night I preached a message from Joshua concerning the Promised Land. We have a responsibility, I said, to take back from the enemy the areas he has stolen from God's people. At my invitation, the front of the church was packed with people giving their lives and businesses to God.

George and I were to leave early Saturday evening on a six-hour drive to Temuco, where we would close out our weekend of ministry. But again the altar was crowded with people crying out to God for deliverance. It was after 11 p.m. when we got started for Temuco.

A Short Night

Needless to say, we didn't get much sleep that night. At the conclusion of the morning service in Temuco, again hundreds of people crowded forward seeking deliverance and healing. We were scheduled to speak in another church Sunday evening. The service began at 5 p.m., and we didn't leave the church until 1:30 a.m.! Our heads were spinning. So many experiencing God's deliverance power. So many accepting His cleansing from sin. So many being saved. God was doing something far larger than our faith had anticipated!

We decided to stay an extra night, so we changed our return tickets. Church began at 7 p.m. Again there was a large response. We left the church at 2 a.m.!

Before George and I started to Chile, we had claimed the words in Acts 4:31 for our trip: "After [the believers] prayed, the place where they were meeting was shaken. And they were all filled with the Holy Spirit and spoke the word of God boldly." Each evening our gathering place "was shaken" with God's power. People were being filled with the Holy Spirit. Everyone spoke the Word of God boldly.

Another Scripture seemed to us very appropriate as well. God says,

> I will go before you
>   and will level the mountains;
> I will break down gates of bronze
>   and cut through bars of iron.
> I will give you the treasures of darkness,
>   riches stored in secret places,
> so that you make know that I am the LORD,
>   the God of Israel, who summons you by name.
>
> (Isaiah 45:2-3)

God Had Broken Through

God in reality had broken through, shattering doors of bronze. He was cutting through the iron bars that Satan had placed around the Temuco Christians and their families. When people were delivered from bondage, they were free to worship and serve God with boldness.

The next morning George and I met with the church leaders in Temuco. They all agreed that this was a "God moment for Chile." What was happening in the city was neither planned nor programmed. It was a divine appointment with God. God was responding to the years of prayer and fasting by many Christians for revival in the church.

George and I agreed to stay the week, holding meetings every night. On Sunday afternoon we would end with a great praise celebration.

Everywhere we went that week—homes, hospitals, offices, the Bible seminary, the Christian radio station—God moved in. He met His people. We witnessed over 200 healings and hundreds of deliverances from demonic powers. At least 40 people prayed for salvation. Hundreds of Christians were dramatically and wonderfully filled with the Holy Spirit. We saw the power of God unleashed in Chile.

Psalm 107:19-21 says it well:

> Then they cried to the LORD in their trouble,
>   and he saved them from their distress.
> He sent forth his word and healed them;
>   he rescued them from the grave.
> Let them give thanks to the LORD for his
>   unfailing love
>   and his wonderful deeds for men.

Not Limited Geographically

What I have personally witnessed in West Africa and more recently in Chile is not limited to those countries. God's healing power through Jesus Christ is being unleashed around the world. He wants to visit nations, all peoples. He wants to visit your friends and family. Will you join with me in believing faith? Will you take God's Word as it stands? Step out in His power, covered by Jesus' blood, protected by God's armor, empowered by the Holy Spirit.

In our own little corner of the world, let us see the strongholds of Satan torn down in Jesus' name. Let us see the demonic forces destroyed that are warring against our churches and our communities.

Let us see revival and healing in all the land as we intercede in faith.

Missions and the Coming Christ

CHAPTER

13

by Wendell K. Grout

WE ALWAYS CHERISH THE LAST WORDS and events associated with the departure of a loved one. When someone dear to us is taking his or her final leave, there is no chit-chat, no idle talk. Everything spoken and done in those last moments we hold in our hearts to be remembered always.

That is one reason why the first 11 verses of Acts has always had special meaning for the followers of the Lord Jesus. Luke, the human author, has preserved for us Jesus' closing words of instruction before He left this world. In a very informal discourse, Jesus encapsulates all the essentials for His disciples' immediate, intermediate and ultimate future. There is no guesswork as to what the Lord Jesus will do for them, what they will do for Him and how it will all turn out.

Observe with me the *prologue*, the *promise*, the *prohibition*, the *plan* and the *prospect*.

The Prologue—Acts 1:1-3

In my former book, Theophilus, I wrote about

all that Jesus began to do and to teach until the day he was taken up to heaven, after giving instructions through the Holy Spirit to the apostles he had chosen. After his suffering, he showed himself to these men and gave many convincing proofs that he was alive. He appeared to them over a period of forty days and spoke about the kingdom of God.

Luke introduces the book we call The Acts of the Apostles with words of immense importance. He says that in his former treatise—the Gospel of Luke—he recorded all that Jesus *began* to do and teach. The implication is that Jesus did not finish His work and teaching in the compass of those 33 recorded years. The further implication is that Luke in this his second treatise will tell of Jesus' ongoing work. Thus the Acts is not so much what the apostles and others are doing for the Lord as *what the Lord is doing through them.* It is not a history of human exploits but rather the exploits of the risen Christ in His people.

Jesus has two bodies. In His physical body He lived on earth for some 33 years. In that body He taught and healed and ministered to people of all classes and at every level of human need. In that body He went to the cross and died in agony for the sins of the whole world. That body was buried and three days later it arose from the dead. Jesus appeared to His own. For 40 days He ministered to His disciples, and then He ascended back to His Father.

In His other, mystical body, Jesus is still on earth. In several places Paul defines and describes this body. He tells us that Jesus is the Head of this body and that all believers are members of this body. In this body we share in common the dynamic life and presence of Jesus Christ. He is just as present now in His mystical body as He was present in His physical body 4 B.C. to A.D. 30. And because of this, He continues to preach and teach and minister to people just as He did during His physical presence on earth. The difference? We are now His eyes and lips and hands and feet. In us His work goes on. That is really the story of Acts—and beyond to this very day.

The Promise—Acts 1:4-5

> *And being assembled together with them, [Jesus] commanded them not to depart from Jerusalem, but to wait for the Promise of the Father, "which," He said, "you have heard from Me; for John truly baptized with water, but you shall be baptized with the Holy Spirit not many days from now."* (NKJV)

For 40 days after His resurrection, Jesus was with His disciples. His presence did two things. It established in an unmistakable manner that He really was alive. It also gave Him further opportunity to instruct His disciples regarding the kingdom. He was preparing them for the work they would do after He was physically removed from them.

Before Jesus tells them what to do, He tells them what not to do. They were not to depart from Jerusalem for any reason until after they had received "the gift my Father promised." They were to *wait* before they were to *work*. It would be presumptuous of them to do anything until after they had received the Promise.

The Promise obviously was not a verbal assurance of some kind. Rather, it was a Person—the Holy

Spirit. In the upper room Jesus had spoken rather extensively about the Holy Spirit (John 14-16). He referred to Him as the Counselor, the One called alongside to help. He had told the disciples that this wonderful Guest would come to them and establish a most intimate relationship with them. Indeed, He would not only dwell *with* them but would actually live *in* them. Thus they would not be left as orphans when Jesus departed.

Probably by this time the disciples were beginning to make some sense out of our Lord's puzzling statement. He had said it would be to their advantage if He went away. He would leave and the Father then would send the Holy Spirit. Now they were beginning to see that He would never leave them spiritually, only physically. In the Promise of the Father, the Holy Spirit, He would come to each of them and take up His dwelling within them. No longer would He have just an external relationship with them. Furthermore, His relationship would no longer be one to eleven; it would now be one to one.

This would be a great advantage. In His physical body, Jesus could only be in one place at a time. Obviously, the disciples had to be where He was at any given moment if they were to see Him or hear Him. But after they received the Promise, the Holy Spirit of Christ, Jesus would be equally with each one, wherever that one might be.

This phenomenon is undoubtedly the explanation for the staggering statement Jesus made to His disciples in the upper room. He said that after His departure the disciples would "do what I have been doing." In fact, they would do "even greater things" (John 14:12). Jesus seems to be saying that by His Spirit the disciples would accomplish the same *quality* of work. In addition, the work would be greater in *quantity* because Jesus was multiplying Himself 11 times! In those 11 men He could go 11 different directions and work in 11 different ways, all at the same time!

Jesus said the Promise would come shortly. Ten days later, the Holy Spirit of Christ descended upon the disciples at Pentecost. There they received His baptism. There the Church, the Body of Christ, was formed (Acts 1; 1 Corinthians 12:13).

The Prohibition—Acts 1:6-7

> So when they met together, they asked him, "Lord, are you at this time going to restore the kingdom to Israel?"
>
> He said to them, "It is not for you to know the times or dates the Father has set by his own authority."

As we have observed, part of Jesus' teaching during the 40 days following His resurrection concerned the kingdom. The disciples understood that the kingdom was here and now in a spiritual sense. And it was future in its messianic and millennial dimensions. The big question in the minds of the disciples was when this future kingdom would be established.

All devout Jews expected the glorious kingdom promised by the prophets would come someday. They looked for the Messiah who would deliver them from their enemies. He would sit in solitary splendor upon His throne and rule over all the nations of the earth.

As Jews, they also believed they would share in

the glory of that great day. The 11 men posing the question had heard Jesus Himself speak of His return to earth (Matthew 24-25; Luke 21:8-38). James and John may have recalled ruefully their mother's request that her sons be seated on His left and right.

It is instructive that Jesus did not discourage His disciples' hope for this great future event. He did not say they should give up the idea of a literal earthly kingdom and the restoration of Israel as a nation. Rather, He prohibits their speculating as to *when* the kingdom will come. This, He says, is privileged information known only to the Father. "The secret things belong to the LORD our God . . ." (Deuteronomy 29:29).

Despite Jesus' pointed prohibition, the church has been plagued through all its history by date-setters. Men and women have concocted complex and fanciful formulas to predict the exact time that Christ will return. Really, it is the height of arrogance—as well as folly—to profess to know what only God knows!

The Plan—Acts 1:8

> But you will receive power when the Holy Spirit comes on you; and you will be my witnesses in Jerusalem, and in all Judea and Samaria, and to the ends of the earth.

The Lord Jesus moves His postresurrection teaching to a stirring climax. Looking into the faces of men who, just weeks before, had so miserably failed Him, He said, "You will receive power when the Holy Spirit comes on you; and you will be my witnesses in Jerusalem, and in all Judea and Samaria, and to the ends of the earth."

Astonishing words! Astonishing when we consider the weak and vulnerable people to whom they were spoken. We remember Philip's dullness and Peter's denials and Thomas's doubts and the cowardly desertion of them all when Jesus needed them most. And yet, Jesus says He is giving them the most important assignment any group ever received. He says He is entrusting to them the greatest work any company ever did. Their future will be taken up entirely in the fulfillment of this, God's great plan. They and the plan of God are inseparably connected. Awesome implications!

William Barclay, in his *Daily Bible Study Series* (*The Gospel of John*, Vol. 2, revised edition, page 212) has these interesting remarks about the disciples:

> *Let us remember who and what they were. A great commentator said: "Eleven Galilean peasants after three years' labor! But it is enough for Jesus, for in these eleven he beholds the pledge of the continuance of God's work upon earth." When Jesus left this world, he did not seem to have great grounds for hope. He seemed to have achieved so little and to have won so few, and it was the great and the orthodox and the religious of the day who had turned against him. But Jesus had that confidence which springs from God. He was not afraid of small beginnings. He was not pessimistic about the future. He seemed to say: "I have won only eleven very ordinary men; but give me these eleven ordinary men and I will change the world."*

Observe the *how* of the plan. "But you will receive power when the Holy Spirit comes on you." A new dynamism will enter the disciples at Pentecost when the power of the Holy Spirit comes on them. In Peter the change is most dramatic. The once stumbling, erratic disciple becomes an instrument of God's authority in a most obvious way. He preached with power (Acts 2:14-41; 3:12-4:12). He healed with power (Acts 3:1-11; 9:32-35). He stood strong against severe opposition (Acts 4:19-22). He prayed with power (Acts 4:23-31). He even saw Dorcas raised from the dead by the power of God (Acts 9:40-42). What a marvelous transformation the Holy Spirit made in Peter's life! The Lord Jesus was working through Peter just as He promised.

Notice, too, the *what* of the plan. "You will be my witnesses." Jesus did not say, "You shall witness." He said, "You will be my witnesses." The emphasis is on *being*, not *doing*. As with Peter, so all of Christ's men would be wonderfully changed and made into witnesses. They would become people of character and ability that they never had been before. At the very beginning of His ministry, Jesus said to those He called, "Come, follow me . . . and I will make you fishers of men" (Mark 1:17). Now it would actually happen!

Finally, look at the *where* of the plan: ". . . in Jerusalem, and in all Judea and Samaria, and to the ends of the earth." They would start where they were and move out to the very ends of the earth. It was not a national plan limited to the Jews. It was an international plan for the whole world. It had universal dimensions. All of this was in keeping with what Jesus had said earlier about preaching repentance and the remission of sins "to all nations, beginning at Jerusalem" (Luke 24:47). There was no mistaking what He said or what He meant.

Slowly at first, but finally the great concept of God's plan to evangelize the whole world caught on. The church in Jerusalem moved out to the "regions beyond." Philip went to Samaria; Peter, to the Gentile centurion, Cornelius; Paul, almost to the ends of the western Roman Empire.

The Prospect—Acts 1:9-11

> After [Jesus] said this, he was taken up before their very eyes, and a cloud hid him from their sight.
>
> They were looking intently up into the sky as he was going, when suddenly two men dressed in white stood beside them. "Men of Galilee," they said, "why do you stand here looking into the sky? This same Jesus, who has been taken from you into heaven, will come back in the same way you have seen him go into heaven."

After the Lord Jesus uttered His final words, He began to ascend heavenward before the eyes of His dumbfounded followers. They stood transfixed as they watched their Lord and Savior move slowly up and disappear into a cloud. Gone! The Man whom they loved and served for three miracle-filled years was gone.

The surrealism of those moments was compounded as "two men dressed in white" suddenly stood beside them. Doubtless they were angels in human form. Their message was a mix of joy and hope and comfort and bright promise. "This same Jesus, who has been taken from you into heaven, will come back in the same way you have seen him go into heaven."

Great things are sometimes compressed into only a few electric moments. The disciples had just seen Jesus ascending into the sky. Now, seconds later, they are told that He is to return! They haven't fully processed the meaning of His ascension when they are told by the heavenly messengers to expect His reappearance! They have just tried to absorb God's plan for their immediate and intermediate future, and now they are given the prospects for their ultimate future!

Concerning the prospects of Jesus' return, what are we to learn from these angelic words?

He will come *personally*. "This same Jesus," the angels promised.

He will come *literally* and *visibly*. ". . . will come back in the same way you have seen him go into heaven." They watched as He ascended. A cloud enfolded Him. "Look, he is coming with the clouds . . ." (Revelation 1:7). "The Lord himself will come down from heaven . . ." (1 Thessalonians 4:16). "He will appear a second time . . . to bring salvation to those who are waiting [watching, NEB] for him" (Hebrews 9:28).

The apostles—and the church born through their ministry—have a ministry. It is a ministry that is to take place between the Lord's ascension and His second advent. Between His going and His coming.

How Does This Apply to Me?

Prologue. Promise. Prohibition. Plan. Prospect. All in the framework of Acts 1:1-11.

Prologue. What Jesus began in His physical body, He now continues in His mystical body, the church. As a member of that body, He can work through me.

Promise. The Holy Spirit, the Promise of the Father, is essential in my life if I am to experience Christ's presence. He is essential if I am to do the works He said His disciples would do. The Acts is an unfinished book, an incomplete history of what Jesus is doing through His people. May He continue the thrilling account through me!

Prohibition. Regarding the Lord's return and the establishment of His kingdom, I must not engage in vain speculation or date setting. Jesus said it is not for us to know the time. I must accept that word. I must leave the timing with my Heavenly Father.

Plan. Amid my weakness and failure, I am to trust the Holy Spirit to empower me. May I become, by His help, a genuine and effective witness for Jesus. I am greatly encouraged as I look at what he did with Peter!

Prospect. This is not a time for gazing at the heavens in idle curiosity. Rather, it is a time for pursuing God's plan to get the gospel to the ends of the earth. Time is passing quickly. Jesus is coming soon.

"Amen. Come, Lord Jesus."

Partners
in
Missions

Missions as *Koinonia* Partnership

by K. Neill Foster

CHAPTER

14

A S YOUNG MEN, WILLIAM JONES AND I were going to make our fortunes hauling gravel. So we bought a gravel truck and got to work. More precisely, we bought an ancient Dodge cab and chassis and began scrounging high and low for a gravel box to mount on the frame. We finally located one. But we faced another problem. Its hydraulic system did not work. We had a gravel truck that could not dump its load! Being youthful and aggressive, we found and bought another gravel box (with a working lift) and kept going.

As up and coming entrepreneurs, we obviously had to put our names on the side of the truck. *JONES and FOSTER*. A young colleague cared for that detail. On the royal blue cab door he laid down a large splotch of white paint reminiscent of an elephant's ear. On that white background he painted—in royal blue letters—our names. Inevitably we called the tired truck "Old Elephant Ear."

Our first hauling job was for a highway construction project. We were one of many trucks loading gravel at the river and transporting it a number of miles to the highway construction site. Full of anticipation, we loaded up at the river, made it up the "dead haul," as they called it, then over the scales and onto the highway. Then to the highway dump site. Our truck was directly behind that of another entrepreneur. He couldn't wait for us to drop our load. He backed into us, doing extensive damage to the front end of our truck.

While the other truckers were making their fortunes, we were making repairs!

But never mind. We did make the repairs and returned to the river to haul our second load. Incredibly, the same thing happened. Again, the trucker ahead was too eager. This time the damage was less, but the radiator was history.

Once more, while others made money, we spent money.

One of our next loads was an overload. I was not along. William my partner knew as he started up the dead haul that he was too heavy. So before he reached the scales he pulled to one side and began to shovel excess gravel over the river bank.

It seemed like a good idea. But it wasn't. The contractor happened along just then and fired us!

After a long wait, we finally got another hauling job. There were no more accidents, but there were incidents. Like when we took out the motor. Like when the rear differential housing collapsed, dropping our truck, stranded, in the middle of the "dead haul" road.

My early partnership experience, as you can tell, was not altogether positive. Both William and I survived it. But William would have been better off had he found a partner without the call of God upon him for ministry.

He and I did learn perseverance and how to handle adversity. In the end, when we sold the truck, we prevailed financially. But the lessons were powerful and tough.

Speaking of Lessons . . .

Speaking of lessons, Philippians is a dramatic and powerful texrbook on missionary work. Bible books can and should be studied in various perspectives. For example, Philippians is one of Paul's "prison" letters. It has a dominant theme of *joy.* But for this chapter of *Missionary Voices,* I want to consider it as a missionary document. Particularly, I am fascinated by Paul's repeated use of the word *koinonia.*

We've come to equate the word *koinonia* with cookies and cake, or maybe coffee and potluck. But in Paul's usage it goes far beyond such social fellowship. "Partnership" is a better translation, but it is more. It is a profound, full-orbed partnership. The Holy Spirit has inspired Paul to show us that the missionary enterprise is intended to be a full partnership in every sense. The insights are powerful.

1. *Koinonia* Is Full Partnership in the Gospel

Paul says, "I thank my God every time I remember you. In all my prayers for all of you, I always pray with joy because of your partnership [*koinonia*] in the gospel from the first day until now, being confident of this, that he who began a good work in you will carry it on to completion until the day of Christ Jesus" (1:3-6).

Paul became joyful when he focused his prayers on the believers at Philippi. The reason was their missionary partnership. There is no doubt that their "partnership in the gospel" was a partnership in the message of the gospel. Their commitment to the gospel was ongoing. It had lasted from the very first days of their acquaintance "until now." Paul also saw this partnership in message as something that, having begun, would show progression and, ultimately, completion.

In another of his letters, Paul elaborates upon his gospel. His message was clear: "Christ did not send me to baptize, but to preach the gospel—not with words of human wisdom, lest the cross of Christ be emptied of its power." He goes on to say, "For the message of the cross is foolishness to those who are perishing, but to us who are being saved it is the power of God" (1 Corinthians 1:17-18).

In the Philippian context I hear Paul saying, "Those Macedonian believers are full partners with me, *koinonia* partners, in the message I am proclaiming."

2. *Koinonia* Is Full Partnership in Grace

Paul had a settled conviction about the Philippians' faithfulness. "Whether I am in chains or defending and confirming the gospel, all of you share [*koinonia*] in God's grace with me" (1:7). Not only was the partnership focused on God's grace, but adherence to grace was connected to its defense.

Sometimes we forget that the preaching of the gospel inevitably stirs up error. Error in fact emerges as a reaction to the hearing of the truth. In Kinshasa, the teeming capital of Zaire, there are thousands of Christian churches. Twenty years ago, a Kinshasa pastor estimated there were 400 false prophets in the city. How many might he estimate today? I can only guess.

Apologetics is nearly as old as Christianity itself. Jude says, "I felt I had to write and urge you to contend for the faith that was once for all entrusted to the saints." Paul understood that error was one of the first reactions to the preaching of the gospel. He warned Timothy that heresy was sure to follow truth (1 Timothy 4:1-3). Happily, Paul felt the full partnership of the Philippians in his defense of the gospel.

Missionary partnership must include an appreciation for apologetics and a willingness to defend the message from the very first day of its proclamation. The common reaction of the counter-kingdom is resistance to the good news. All opposition requires an honorable and intelligent defense. Paul's good fortune as a missionary was that from the very beginning of his relationship with the Philippians, they had partnered with him in defending the faith.

Defending the gospel in those days entailed risk. It could easily mean the executioner's block. But Paul was not a lone defender of the faith. He was strengthened by the *koinonia* of his brothers and sisters in Philippi.

3. *Koinonia* Is Full Partnership in Confirmation.

The Christian gospel can be confirmed. "The disciples went out and preached everywhere, and the Lord worked with them and confirmed his word by the signs that accompanied it" (Mark 16:20). There are similar words in the Letters: "This salvation, which was first announced by the Lord, was confirmed to us by those who heard him. God also testified to it by signs, wonders and various miracles, and gifts of the Holy Spirit distributed according to his will" (Hebrews 2:3-4). "Christ has become a servant of the Jews on behalf of God's truth, to confirm the promises made to the patriarchs" (Romans 15:8).

Paul makes it clear that the Philippians "share God's grace" with him, whether he was "in chains or defending and confirming the gospel" (Philippians 1:7). This partnership or *koinonia* in the confirming of the gospel is a fascinating detail in Paul's missiology. Paul and Silas had not been in Philippi long when they met the demented slave girl. When they abruptly drove out the demon (coincidentally confirming their ministry), they started a riot. God wasn't caught off guard by such eruptions. Earthquakes and open prison doors and a repenting jailer only served to provide additional confirmation to the apostles' message!

Much later, when Paul was shipwrecked on the isle of Malta, a viper fixed itself to his hand. Not to worry. He shook it into the fire and suffered no harm. More confirmation! The incident led to a ministry of healing that reached a public official. Confirmation of the message and the messenger can be very exciting business in the advance of Christ's kingdom!

The Philippians understood and well remembered the events recorded in Acts 16. Similarly, the islanders of Malta responded with *koinonia* partnership as the Holy Spirit confirmed Paul's ministry. Luke says, "They honored us in many ways and when we were ready to sail, they furnished us with the supplies we needed" (Acts 28:10).

When Norman and Marie Enns were wartime missionaries in Cambodia, danger was everywhere. Without warning explosives fell in the streets. The physical safety of their children was a constant concern. In that context Marie writes:

One day a postcard arrived from . . . Bangkok.
The picture said it all. A tender hand was out-
stretched, the fingers curved gently upward. In the
hollow of the hand sat a tiny fragile chick
crouched in absolute fearlessness, its wee feet
tucked under its delicate body. Clear bright eyes
gazed out unconcernedly. And underneath, the
caption read, "Be not afraid! Only believe! Your
Father cares for you!"

But that was not all. Marie continues:

Within days an identical message arrived from a
young Cambodian who was studying in Paris. His
postcard read, "Be not afraid. You are in God's
hands." [It was] another confirming communica-
tion from the Lord assuring His trusting children
of His tender care for them.

Surely the confirming *koinonia* partnership in
grace that the Philippians enjoyed with Paul is
reciprocal with the Holy Spirit as well. He confirms
His Word by events and circumstances in the lives
of His partnering people.

4. *Koinonia* Is Full Partnership in Gospel Advance

Paul's prison experience was related in his mind
to the advance of the gospel. "Now I want you to
know, brothers, that what has happened to me has
really served to advance the gospel" (Philippians
1:12). The partnership in defense and the confirmation of the gospel (1:7) seems now to extend to
gospel advance.

The intimation is clear. Gospel advance is the essence of the Christian message. If missions is indeed

spiritual warfare (and it is), then the Great Commission is a declaration of war against the counter-kingdom. *Koinonia* is locking into partnership with the advance of the Christian message. A *koinonia* Christian is one whose interest in reaching the world is partnered with those on the front lines of missionary endeavor.

One of my most memorable sights was at Bongolo in the heart of Gabon on Africa's equator. Soaring into the sky, literally in the center of the jungle, was an immense tin-roofed church. It had been erected by Donald Fairley, a pioneer missionary to Gabon. I wondered what kind of a man he was.

Later it was my privilege to meet Don and Dorothy Fairley in Oregon. Face to face with this man and his wife, I was surprised by two things. I was surprised that Don was so small of stature—not much over five feet tall, as I remember. I was also surprised by their "book of prayer," as they called it. It was a three-ring binder jammed with notes and other writings. Over many years, the Fairleys had kept a record of the prayer requests they had prayed for, along with God's answers.

This little man with an immense vision had, with his family, penetrated northward from Zaire. They had pressed through multiple dangers on into Gabon. Once there, they had planted the church of Jesus Christ.

I can remember Libreville, the capital, when it was without a single evangelical church. More recently I preached at Avea Deux, an immense church that is still expanding in one of Libreville's suburbs. There must have been 2,000 people in the two congregations that gathered in the church building. I will never forget the acrid smell of smoke wafting through the auditorium from the burning of fetishes taking place just outside. It was a regular occurrence at Avea Deux.

There was no human promise of success as Don Fairley dared to advance northward. There were not hundreds of believers to fill the great church soaring skyward at Bongolo. There was no human promise of a great harvest. But still Don Fairley advanced.

Why? It was in his blood and in his bones. But more to the point, it was in his faith, his message, his gospel, his mandate. "Go into all the world and preach the good news to all creation" (Mark 16:15). Don Fairly could do no less than obey.

Today Gabon is experiencing a great ingathering. Churches are multiplying in Libreville and elsewhere. Men and women are forcing their way into the kingdom of God. One of the human reasons is that Don Fairley, missionary entrepreneur, was in profound *koinonia* with the advancing Holy Spirit. The divine reason for Gabon's day of power in these days is that the Holy Spirit has always delighted to partner with every advancing heart.

5. *Koinonia* Is Full Partnership in Suffering

In Philippians 3:10 Paul talks about sharing in the sufferings of Jesus Christ. Certainly it is not popular to talk about suffering, let alone to celebrate one's participation in it. Yet Paul had learned that the *koinonia* of suffering was a doorway to spiritual power. One translation puts it this way: "Faith knows the power that his coming back to life gives and what it means to share his suffering" (GWV). Peter says, "Since Christ suffered in his body, arm yourselves also with the same attitude" (1 Peter 4:1).

Suffering is not a teaching of those promoting a "health and wealth" gospel. Nor should we seek suffering, as some early Christians did by avidly seeking martyrdom. But suffering can and does come. It is as much a part of the kingdom as are the miracles of healing.

Today the Christian church in Zaire, Africa, is pervasive. But in the early days of missions in Zaire (then known as the Congo), an appointment there was almost a death sentence. In those days there was much physical and emotional suffering. At one time there were more missionary graves than living missionaries. Brawny men where cut down, one after another, creating widows in multiples. Husbands laid their wives to rest and plodded on. Fair-haired children were buried in African soil.

The suffering and the pain were beyond endurance—yet the missionaries endured both because *koinonia* partnership in the gospel included suffering. The witness of those early missionaries in Zaire was suffering power. It emerged from a partnership with the Almighty God. That partnership excluded neither the power of the resurrection nor the power of fellowship with Christ in His suffering. And out of the tears and pain of a decimated missionary staff has emerged a great, great church.

The missionaries were in partnership with our Lord in His suffering. But what about us? What about those of us who could be and should be in an ongoing *koinonia* partnership? Might that partnership, too, someday include suffering with those who follow the call to distant fields?

6. *Koinonia* Is Full Partnership in Finance

The Philippian church was the only Macedonian

church to share financially in Paul's missionary endeavors (Philippians 4:15). The apostle makes it clear that he can be content, whatever his financial circumstances. "I know what it is to be in need, and I know what it is to have plenty," he says (4:12). But clearly he is grateful that the Philippian *koinonia* has extended to monetary aid.

Their funding was according to need. "You sent me aid again and again when I was in need," Paul says (4:16). At times it was beyond bare needs. "I have received full payment and even more; I am amply supplied" (4:18). Their gift while Paul was imprisoned was sent through a reputable person, Epaphroditus (4:18). That suggests the need for responsible stewardship in missionary funding. Paul calls their offering "an acceptable sacrifice, pleasing to God" (4:18).

George Mueller, whose legendary faith was used by God to sustain thousands of orphans in Britain, is well-known among Christians. Little known is the fact that Mueller was also a missionary financier. Mueller was a great supporter of Hudson Taylor's China Inland Mission. It would seem that God calls some to be partners in giving just as He calls others to plunge into the thick of battle in the "regions beyond."

The Philippians were *koinonia* partners in their monetary giving to missions. When the Philippian *koinonia* so clearly included finances, are we ever justified to associate this word with an informal time of fun and food? If biblical words like *koinonia* have any meaning at all, this one goes far beyond that.

The Call

The implications of the material we have examined are profound. *Koinonia* is nothing less than full partnership in taking the gospel to the unreached worldwide.

- Full missionary partnership has everything to do with the message of the gospel
- Full missionary partnership has everything to do with the advance of the gospel
- Full missionary partnership has everything to do with the defense of the gospel
- Full missionary partnership has everything to do with the confirmation of the gospel
- Full missionary partnership has everything to do with demonstrating the power of Christ through sharing in His sufferings
- Full missionary partnership is a life-consuming, pervasive financial commitment to missions

The call, then, is for us to be *koinonia* Christians—full partners in the missionary enterprise. The biblical example in Philippians is before us. And a lost world beckons us. "All of you share in God's grace with me," Paul told the Philippians (1:7). They were partners, full partners, in the missionary enterprise.

"Old Elephant Ear." Remember? William and I were true partners. We survived the difficulties. We finally found a buyer for our old, broken-down truck. In the end we prevailed. Ultimately, both of us drove vehicles that had their financial roots in that old Dodge truck and a wholly miserable enterprise. But neither William nor I ever faltered in our partnership.

At this distance it makes for a great story. We ended well, if not well off. William and I are still good friends and the proud owners of a mutual chapter in our lives.

And inevitably, all I see in Scripture about the *koinonia* partnership is colored by the Old Elephant Ear experiences. Indeed, if I understand missionary *koinonia* at all, it may well be because, in God's grace, early on in life I found myself in a partnership!

Missions and Women in Ministry

by Joy E. Corby

WHY IN THIS BOOK IS THERE A CHAPTER entitled "Missions and *Women* in Ministry"? Could it be because women comprise well over 50 percent of the world missionary force? Is it because, historically, women have made a name for themselves in missionary exploits? Maybe it is simply that God has called *all* of us—men and women—to the ministry of reconciliation (see 2 Corinthians 5:18).

The ministry of reconciliation involves far more than just proclaiming the gospel (though we women may have a reputation for being verbal). It involves life and example. As new creations, reconciled to God, we have had conferred on us "the ministry of reconciliation." Not only the men. But men and women. We—men and women—are Christ's ambassadors (5:20). God communicates to people through us.

The focus here, as the *Theological Dictionary of the New Testament* points out, is not on the ambassadors—us. The ambassadors simply convey the message. The focus is on the authority of the message. All of us, men *and* women, are responsible to

178

exalt God and make His will known on earth. That is the ministry Christ has left to us. We are called to be His witnesses, His partners, His ambassadors.

Some of us women have felt called to this ministry of reconciliation in a cross-cultural context. We ourselves have experienced God's reconciliation, peace and comfort. We have responded by going forth as His ambassadors, announcing the good news of reconciliation.

Coequal in Ministry

Isaiah said, "The Spirit of the Sovereign LORD is on me, / because the LORD has anointed me / to preach good news to the poor. / He has sent me to bind up the brokenhearted, / to proclaim freedom for the captives / and release from darkness for the prisoners" (Isaiah 61:1). I have seen firsthand those who have been held in severe bondage by Satan and his demons.

I have ministered side by side with others—missionaries and Gabonese—as we prayed for complete deliverance for new believers in Christ. Simply by using the name of Jesus I have heard demons shudder (James 2:19). I know from experience that the weapons of our spiritual warfare are powerful. "They have divine power to demolish strongholds" (2 Corinthians 10:4). I have also seen firsthand the display of God's love, comfort and peace.

From the Beginning, Women

From New Testament times on, women have played an important role in missions. As the 19th century and the era of modern missions opened, most of the missionaries were men. But as Ruth A.

Tucker observes in her landmark book, *From Jerusalem to Irian Jaya,*

> *Many of these men had wives. The wives served faithfully alongside their husbands, but they were not generally viewed as missionaries in their own right. By the end of the century, however, the situation was vastly different. Single women had begun pouring into foreign missionary service, and married women were beginning to assume a more active role. No longer was foreign missions a male profession.* (pages 228-234)

Some missionaries' wives have been extremely dedicated. Others have just "gone along." Many single women have been attracted to missionary service because it offers them greater opportunities for ministry. Frequently the cost has been loneliness and difficulties. Regardless, both single and married women have played a vital role in missions.

My Missionary Grandmother, Elma Hess Mason

My grandmother, Elma Hess, was saved in 1900 at the age of 18 during a Salvation Army meeting. Her family attended a missions-minded church in Hesston, Pennsylvania. There God called her to Africa.

So strong was her sense of call that Grandmother broke off her engagement to prepare for overseas service. Nothing would deter her from her goal. Not even another prospective husband in the student body, David Mason, who also was committed to Africa. In 1913, David—unattached—sailed for what is now Zaire. Elma followed a year later.

Grandmother's ministry that first year included teaching and evangelism. Before the year was out, she became engaged to David. The mission under which they served had very strict rules about marriage. But because my grandfather had already been in Zaire two years, they were permitted to marry in 1915—just a year after Grandmother had arrived. Together the two of them served in itinerant evangelism and teaching in the Bible school that David began.

When children came, things changed. At that time, children were not permitted to accompany their missionary parents. During their second term, my grandparents left their two older children with David's sister in Scotland. But a third child came during that second term of service, and a fourth was on the way as their second term ended. Grandmother reasoned that God had given her and her husband those four children, and she refused to abandon them to others. When they returned home in 1923, it was to continue their ministry for God in North America.

Meet My Missionary Mother

The oldest child of David and Elma Mason is my mother, Betty Corby. Mother was not at all bitter about being left in Scotland while her parents served in Zaire. When she was nine years old, a Black man visited the family. He knew that my mother had been born in Africa.

"You must return to your country to take the gospel to your people," he exhorted her. It was the beginning of Mother's missionary call, a call that persisted and deepened. In college she met Bert

Corby, who shared her missionary goal. In 1941 they were married, and two years later they sailed for Gabon. World War II was still raging.

Dad and Mother were involved in Bible translation, dispensary work, literacy classes, itinerant evangelism and teaching. "I never felt restricted!" Mother says of her role as a woman missionary.

While serving in Gabon, Dad and Mother had two children. Both my brother John and I are third generation missionaries. Both of us served in Gabon. More recently John and his wife, Fran, have been working in France.

Two by Two in Ministry

Both Mark (6:7) and Luke (10:1) inform us that Jesus sent out His disciples in pairs. In foreign missionary service, such a "pair" has historically and normally been marriage partners. But for the unmarried missionary, a ministry partner of the same gender is preferable to being alone. At least, I am of that opinion. The standard procedure is for field leaders to *assign* same-gender pairs to a particular location. Not always have field leaders exercised sensitivity in such pairing. After all, if marriage partners are matched carefully and prayerfully, should not ministry partners be assigned with equal care and sensitivity? Why not try to achieve the best possible working match among the singles? Perhaps we singles need to pray that God will at least send us a good ministry partner.

For His own reasons, God did not provide me with a marriage partner. But he did provide a ministry partner! It happened while both of us were in French language study. Becky was not even under the same mission board as I, nor was she assigned to Gabon. God, however, in a very short period of time, miraculously orchestrated events to bring about our partnership. Becky and I lived and ministered together until her marriage in April, 1993.

A New Challenge in Partnership

The final year of our first term in Gabon, Becky and I continued our assignment in Libreville. But the field leaders asked us to live with Julie Fehr, 18 years our senior, who was returning to Gabon after studies during furlough. All three of us sensed the difficulty of the situation, but we determined to make it work. We made a point of praying and sharing with one another every day. That prayer time served also to unite us. At the end of the year, Becky and I had become close friends with Julie. Our friendship continued until God called Julie to her heavenly home.

All of us—missionaries and supporting Christians in the homeland—have been reconciled to God. We have been given a ministry of reconciliation. Certainly we need to keep the channels clear between ourselves and our fellow Christians. Jesus implied as much when He said to those whose "brothers" might have something against them, "First go and be reconciled to your brother; then come and offer your gift" (Matthew 5:24). If we are having difficulty in relationships, we will have difficulty in ministry.

When Conflicts Arise in Ministry

We all need more skill when it comes to resolving conflicts. Perhaps that applies especially to missionaries, and even more to single women in missionary ministry. More than once I "ate humble pie" in order to be reconciled with a fellow missionary. (I must admit that sometimes I put it off as long as possible!)

There is another dimension of reconciliation. We must be reconciled to ourselves. Matthew Henry makes the point in his commentary on God's admonition to Israel to "love your neighbor as yourself" (Leviticus 19:18). The dictum was repeated by Jesus more than once. He called it the second greatest commandment (Matthew 22:39). But there is also a "reverse" implication to the command. It implies that we must accept ourselves for who we are. We must have concern for our own welfare and bodies. We must have dignity for our own natures. When we are at odds with ourselves, we will have trouble relating with others.

All of us these days seem to be carrying a backpack of unresolved problems and cumbersome burdens. Missionaries are no exception. Once overseas, stripped of the familiar support, they are especially vulnerable. I remember that during language study I discovered what really was within me. And I was not at all pleased with what I saw! With self-determination and God's help, I made changes. We all can make changes, though some are harder to make than others.

When the Assignment Is Disappointing

It was April, 1987. I was within months of completing a year-long missionary furlough from Gabon. At the time I was visiting my parents. With me was Becky, my longtime friend and missionary partner in Gabon.

The telephone rang. It was a long-distance call for me from our field chairman in Gabon. For our up-coming term, would Becky and I consider an assignment to Mounana, a small mining town, to replace a retiring couple?

Becky and I were anticipating a return to Libreville, one of the large cities in Gabon. We had made our preparations accordingly. This abrupt change of direction was hard to understand. It troubled us. Both of us expressed our hesitation to the field chairman, but we agreed to give it prayerful consideration.

Neither Becky nor I could fully understand the reasoning behind this change of plans for our ministry. But both of us, as we waited on God, came to feel that Mounana was indeed where God wanted us upon our return to Gabon. We notified the field chairman of our willingness to be assigned there.

Eternally Grateful

I had not wanted to go to Mounana, but I'm glad I did! As Becky and I continued to work there, I began to experience what *partnership* was all about. There was, of course, my continuing partnership with Becky. But there was also partnership with Raymond and Maurine Holcomb, missionary colleagues. There were Marie and Agnes, Gabonese sisters in Christ. There was Gilles, our Gabonese prayer partner, and Jean Marcel, a Gabonese who took my place in extension education. There was Pierre, who took on the bookstore ministry, and Bakimbi, who became a youth leader. There was Rosine, one of my spiritual children who reproduced herself wherever she went. And many others.

My life has been enriched by these relationships. For them I will be eternally grateful.

As we began the final year of that term in Mounana, Becky and I knew the mission did not plan to assign other personnel to that town. We became even more intent on training our Gabonese partners to replace us. By the time we left, every ministry for which we had been responsible was under Gabonese leadership. And without missionary presence the Mounana church continued to grow. A year later, attendance was reported to be 800!

A few months before I left Mounana, I was in the midst of my private devotions. Almost out of the blue, the Lord let me know why He had directed me to that out-of-the-way mining town. Yes, I had been involved in teaching, in training, in discipleship. But there was something greater. "Put on the full armor of God," I read, "so that when the day of evil comes, you may be able to stand your ground, and after you have done everything, to stand" (Ephesians 6:13). *Stand your ground. Stand.* In the next verse, *Stand firm.* Our responsibility had been to "stand firm" for Christ and His Word. As we stood firm, God had enabled us to "proclaim [Christ], admonishing and teaching everyone with all wisdom, so that we may present everyone perfect [complete] in Christ" (Colossians 1:28).

As partners, we *all* stood together. Although I am no longer physically there, I continue to be a partner with my Gabonese brothers and sisters. We are *all* partners as we stand together!

	Missions and
CHAPTER	**the Family**
16	
	by Paul F. Bubna

WORLD MISSIONS DEMANDS MIS-
SIONARIES. Churches and missionary
organizations are faced with the source
question. Where will the missionaries come from?
What educational institutions have influenced their
lives? What kind of local churches have shaped
their view of ministry? What family experiences
have molded their character and disciplined their
lives?

It is the last of these questions that I want to address.
How does what is happening in the family ultimately
influence the mission of the church in the world?

My wife Jeanie and I had the joy of raising five
children, all of whom are kingdom people. Two are
in pastoral ministry here in North America, two are
planting churches in other cultures and one is
equally a kingdom person in lay ministry. People
ask me what influenced our children in their life in-
vestment choices.

Those who inquire often assume there is something parents do to help this happen. (We are quick
to look for a program or a gimmick to get the

results we are after!) I think our children would all say their father and mother did not *specifically* encourage them to pursue pastoral or missionary work. It is not an accident, however, that there were both grandparents and great-grandparents who modeled kingdom commitment. I am convinced that the values lived out in the family *do* influence the children. And they influence, positively or negatively, the mission of the church in the world.

Missions and the Trinity

As with all questions of substance, we need to begin with God. The first decision to send a missionary was made long before creation. It took place in a family setting. The apostle Paul writes:

> Praise be to the God and Father of our Lord Jesus Christ, who has blessed us in the heavenly realms with every spiritual blessing in Christ. For he chose us in him before the creation of the world *to be holy and blameless in his sight.*"
> (Ephesians 1:3-4, emphasis added)

Before God cast the worlds into orbit, before He made Adam and Eve in His image and placed them in Eden, He had planned a missionary initiative. In His infinite foreknowledge God the Father knew our parents would fall. Before Adam was formed from the dust of the ground, He chose to send a very special Missionary:

> For God so loved the world that he gave his one and only son, that whoever believes in him shall not perish but have eternal life. (John 3:16)

188

The first "Sent One" was the very Son of God. His mission was formed in the Father's heart. It was a family decision to send Jesus Christ, the Son. Preachers and writers have stretched their imaginations, endeavoring to describe that conference of the Godhead. It was a council that addressed an unthinkable choice. God the Son would leave heaven's glory to enter the fallen race of Adam as Mary's Son.

Such speculations may have some value. But they must not substitute for adoring wonder as we stand awed before the mystery of the Trinity. Two facts are sure: One, the Father sent His one and only Son. Two, the Son chose to come.

When the Son chose to be the "Sent One," He was simply displaying the character of His "Family." God is love. It is His nature to be self-sacrificing. Like an infinite centrifugal force, the love of God is ever giving, ever reaching out. The Son came bearing the nature of His Family.

Throughout His ministry, Jesus made it clear that He had been sent and that He was discharging the will of His Father.

> *I tell you the truth, the Son can do nothing by himself; he can do only what he sees his Father doing, because whatever the Father does the Son also does. For the Father loves the Son and shows him all he does.* (John 5:19-20)

Jesus' mission reflected the will and character of His Family. His communication of the gospel to people who otherwise would be lost flows from the fullness and love of the Trinity.

The Great Commission Was Rooted in a Family Covenant

We usually think of the Great Commission as a command Jesus gave His followers shortly before His ascension. In fact, God stated His intention to extend saving grace to all nations in His covenant with Abraham:

> The LORD had said to Abram [Abraham], "Leave your country, your people and your father's household and go to the land I will show you.
>
> "I will make you into a great nation
>   and I will bless you;
> I will make your name great,
>   and you will be a blessing.
> I will bless those who bless you,
>   and whoever curses you I will curse;
> and all peoples on earth
>   will be blessed through you."
>   (Genesis 12:1-3, emphasis added)

God's intention and promise to bless all the families of the earth is clear. Notice that the promise is inextricably tied to God's blessing on Abraham's family. Notice also that God made the promise as He called Abraham to leave his home country and home people. The symbolism is striking.

God's promise to bless Abraham and make him a world blessing hinged on a son he did not have. That son became a faith issue in which Abraham's performance was less than perfect. But in their old age, God gave Abraham and Sarah a son. Isaac was the child of promise through which the blessing would come—to Abraham and to the world.

The eternal Father who before creation chose to send His Son as a sacrifice, asked the same of Abraham (Genesis 22:1-2). This time his obedience was perfect. At the appointed place, in an incredible act of faith, Abraham was ready to sacrifice the son of the promise. Just as Abraham raised his knife, God stopped him, providing a lamb in Isaac's stead. Abraham did not know about God's Son and about Calvary. But God knew. And God saw in Abraham a kindred spirit. Abraham, the man willing to sacrifice his son, became a friend of God, who would sacrifice His Son as a ransom for many.

The Incarnation unfolds in the life of a family. The issues of faith are played out in Joseph's amazing trust and Mary's total surrender to the call of God. Jesus became both Son of man and Son of God.

> *Although he was a son, he learned obedience from what he suffered and, once made perfect, he became the source of eternal salvation for all who obey him.* (Hebrews 5:8-9)

On a Roman cross, the Son of God, the Son of Abraham and David and Mary hung between time and eternity—the Savior. As He breathed out His life in indescribable agony, His human mother stood at the foot of the cross and wept.

The Great Commission Is a Family Issue

The church is to be planted among peoples and in language groups where the gospel is unknown. If that is to happen, someone must climb over the cultural walls and enter those foreign worlds. That someone is part of a human family. Like Abraham, he or she must leave home and homeland. God sacrificed His one and only Son. Over and over, that heavenly drama is played out as the missionary enterprise advances.

Missionaries *do* come from families. Many influences shape their lives—churches, communities, colleges, seminaries. But the home is by far the most important. It is in the home, in the early childhood years, that life-shaping character and inner discipline are learned. Sociological and spiritual changes in North America are having a profound influence on the home—and on the missionary candidate pool.

Until this past generation, most of the missionary activity in the world flowed from Western Europe and North America. Churches in other parts of the world are now catching the missionary impetus. For that we are thankful. At the same time, societal changes in the western world are impacting North America's once-strong missionary thrust.

A century and a half ago, the vast majority of North American children grew up in rural settings. Boys grew up working the fields beside their fathers. Girls shared with their mothers the unending labors of the rural homestead. Missionary candidates came from this sturdy, hardworking stock.

Industrialization and urbanization, followed by two world wars, revolutionized family structures. Fathers set off to work in places often unknown and unseen by their children. Beginning with World War II, mothers followed their husbands to the workplace. Growing mobility erased the extended-family paradigm (grandparents, aunts, uncles, cousins clustered in easy proximity). Instead, it was the nuclear family—and hardly that as accelerating divorce rates made one-parent families increasingly common. In this milieu, building and maintaining a solid family structure are no longer automatic. They must be intentional choices.

There was a day when missionaries were more than likely the sons or daughters of missionaries. (Third-generation missionaries were not uncommon.) This is becoming less and less the case. Increasingly, the missionary pool is made up of men and women who did not grow up in Christian homes and may have had little experience in a local church. This, of course, does not negate their calling. Down through the years, some very effective missionaries have had little or no family encouragement. On the other hand, missionaries, like all of us, are the products of their home environment. What goes on in families has a profound effect upon the missionary enterprise.

Some Personal Reflections

Currently I am president of a seminary. The societal trends I have sketched tend to be reflected in the student population. Last year, along with the students in our leadership class, I wrote a "vision statement" for my life. In doing so, I reaffirmed what I have always known. I am a Great Commission person. Jeanie and I served only briefly in an overseas assignment (the International Protestant Church in Saigon, Vietnam). But my prayer life and thought life and my daily disciplines revolve around missions. Completing the task of world evangelization defines my life. How did this come about?

The short answer is that God called me. The fuller answer includes a number of significant influences, not least being the family I grew up in.

Both my parents were first-generation believers. Each was led to saving faith by a lay person. They became faithful members of a Bible-believing church. They were present for almost every service, including the annual missions conference. Our pastor's passion for missions was a powerful influence on my life. But it was at home that my values were shaped.

The modest home we rented sat on a 25-foot lot. The three rooms in that one-story house were in a straight line. The front room was our parlor. (But at night my brothers and I slept there on a fold-out couch.) The middle room was my parents' bedroom. The back room was the kitchen, with a very small bathroom attached.

Yet in that restricted space, hospitality was a value that my parents clearly lived out. Almost every week we had guests in our home. Very few missionaries visited our church without having a meal at the Bubnas'. Among my friends at school or in my neighborhood, I did not know anyone who had been on an ocean-going ship, and certainly not on an airplane. Yet our home was trafficked by world travelers. As a young boy I sat on the floor and listened to stories of God's work in West Africa, the Near East, Thailand, China, South America. Probably no other children in my elementary school grew up in as big a world as I did.

Like just about everyone during those Depression years, my family lived on a very limited income. Yet I knew my parents not only tithed but made a faith promise to missions over and above that. I can remember my parents guiding me to tithe my weekly allowance and later to make my first faith promise to world missions. They were forming my value system. I do not remember their ever talking to me about being a missionary, but it was very evident that in our family, world evangelization was of highest priority.

I grew up during the closing decades of racial segregation. I remember that my grandmother—my mother's mother—was something of a racist. But my parents never reflected that attitude. After it became too late to ask them, I have often wondered why. Did their world view, born out of missionary hearts, make the difference?

As I tell this story again, I am grateful for what my parents, as new believers, built into my life. I am also keenly aware that this story is not typical—not of that era and certainly not of this one. So where are we?

Some Further Reflections

The growing number of missionary candidates coming from unbelieving homes and with little exposure to the church is troubling. Although it is a problem, churches and other missionary sending agencies need to be realistic about it. They need to take steps to fill in the blanks. We can deal with the problem if we will.

Many of these young people have come to faith because they experienced the emptiness of the materialism pervading our secular culture. Others have been deeply wounded by childhood abuse. They have turned from the emptiness and disappointment of the past to embrace the Way, the

Truth and the Life. God has used those contexts in which they grew up to point them to the kingdom. He has used those experiences to stir their hearts for a world in need of Jesus. Often these young men and women are marked by a refreshing vitality and a kingdom mindset.

Actually, I am more concerned about the youth growing up in our evangelical tradition. They are being shaped by families who attend church and profess to know and follow Christ. But I wonder what kingdom values are being lived out those homes. I wonder what place the Great Commission has in the family's financial decisions and its time priorities. I wonder what message these children are hearing about investing their lives in something of eternal consequence.

I wonder, because 38 years in the pastorate have left me with some impressions. I perceive an unspoken universalism creeping in among us evangelicals. No one dares to say that people can be saved without coming to faith in Christ and His atoning sacrifice. But our choices and priorities are no longer shaped by the compelling conviction that people without Christ are lost—eternally. In practice we live like the universalists who declare God is going to save everyone. That allows us to be comfortable with materialistic goals and life investments that are short term.

No longer is missionary service seen as a compelling call from the Lord of the church. Instead, it is viewed as just another career choice among a myriad. And one not very high on the list at that. I fear many Christian parents would panic should their child choose missionary service instead of medicine or another prestigious profession. It is one thing for young people to have unbelieving parents who do not understand God's call. It is another thing when church-going Christian parents send messages that fly in the face of kingdom values.

Ultimately, being a missionary involves dying to one's own dreams and career goals. It means entering the culture and language of another people. It is a servant role. It is costly. Some, after years of preparation, reach the distant land of their appointment and decide the price is too high. They may have taken up residence in a foreign land, but they are speaking across a wide chasm. They are an unintelligible voice from another world. Servanthood is a kingdom value best learned when it is fleshed out in family life.

Heaven's "Family" Values

Dr. Howard Hendricks, Dallas Theological Seminary, makes an astute observation. He says a child who senses parental love and acceptance will most naturally adopt the parents' value system. Sometimes Christian parents are shocked by the materialistic, worldly values their children express. Could those children be modeling not the dogma their parents taught them, but the values their parents lived out in the home?

From the only perfect "Family," God the Father sent God the Son to model heaven's "Family" values before a fallen world. God the Son set aside His glory, choosing instead to be robed in human flesh. He humbled Himself even further and became a servant. In the end, His great love for humankind took Him to the cross. His atoning sacrifice made possible our adoption into the family of God as sons and daughters.

Over the centuries of church history, God has sent many of these redeemed sons and daughters as His special messengers. He has asked them to climb over the walls of culture and language. He has commissioned them to share the good news of saving grace.

That so many have obeyed so implicitly and served so faithfully should not surprise us. They are children of the Servant-King. They are reflecting Family values!

<table>
<tr><td>

CHAPTER

17
</td><td>

Missions and the Academy

by Norman E. Allison
</td></tr>
</table>

TODAY IS AN EXCITING TIME FOR MISSIONS. Jesus' commission, "As the Father has sent me, I am sending you" (John 20:21), is meeting with response! There is a fresh vitality among Christian young people thrilled by the prospect of serving God among the world's unreached people. And this excitement is not limited to North America!

Unfortunately, as many educators have discovered, excitement often dims with the months and years of hard work necessary for missionary preparation. Many bright prospective candidates are not really aware of the need for academic preparation. Some are zealous to reach the unreached with the gospel. But their concept of preparation for missionary service often involves little more than having a basic Bible knowledge. They are then ready to "launch out" into whatever part of the world they want to evangelize.

Just recently I talked to a high school senior. His was an unusual circumstance. "Since I was eight years old," he told me, "I knew the Lord wanted me to serve Him as a missionary in the jungles of Brazil." He was ready to go right now! Had it not been for godly parents who were counseling him to prepare, he would have been on the next flight to Brazil. But as we talked, he began to realize, grudgingly, that he needed to be ready for the future that God had in mind for him.

A Difficult Task

Missionary educators face a difficult task. They must continue to stimulate this zeal to reach those who have never heard the gospel. At the same time, they must instill knowledge that God can use for cross-cultural communication in a very complex world. To accomplish this dual objective, missionary education today is approached most often from two perspectives.

One is the avenue of *a liberal arts undergraduate education plus seminary*. This usually involves the prospective missionary in an undergraduate major such as psychology, history, English, leading to a bachelor's degree. If the study is done at a Christian liberal arts college, there will be some elective classes in Bible and theology along with chapel services that serve to stimulate spiritual growth. The baccalaureate degree is normally followed by three years of seminary. At the seminary, there is usually a combination of concentrations: biblical studies, missions, anthropology, pastoral studies, philosophy and religion. The seminarian graduates with a Master of Divinity (M.Div.) degree.

This plan for missionary education customarily entails a total of at least seven years of academic studies. Actual ministry preparation is done in the final three years. Some educators believe this structure serves to give the student a broad base of liberal arts necessary to any type of post-secondary education.

The other approach to missionary education is *Bible college plus graduate school*. This option moves the student, at the very beginning of the freshman year, into a track designed for prospective missionaries. In most Bible colleges, the student will receive approximately two years of liberal arts courses rather than four. He or she will also have one year of Bible and theology courses (interspersed throughout the four-year undergraduate process). Other courses are designed to develop skills and knowledge in church growth, missions strategy, cultural anthropology, cross-cultural communication, language acquisition.

The student normally graduates with a Bachelor of Arts degree—the same as his or her counterpart in the liberal arts college. This plan, however, permits the student to begin his or her missionary training in the freshman year. That training builds progressively through to the senior year of college.

For graduate education, this student will likely enter a graduate school (rather than a seminary). He or she will continue to prepare with even greater depth in the areas of ministry and cross-cultural studies. This individual has had already, on the undergraduate level, two years of specialized cross-cultural training and biblical studies. Therefore graduate education is usually only one additional year (30 semester hours) leading to a Master of Arts (M.A.) degree. This second academic option for prospective missionaries involves a total of five years, rather than seven, with ministry studies every year.

As with any model of training, Christian missionary training must be evaluated continually. With rapid changes accelerating in many regions of the world, missionary training must retain its solid biblical and theological core. At the same time, it must be reviewed in light of goals and outcomes necessary for those being trained.

Missionary candidates must be adequately prepared to serve God in the world of the 21st century. To discern key building blocks in the academic preparation of missionary candidates, educators must give attention to four basic areas. Each of these areas of preparation must be incorporated into the training process. They are essential to the structure of the curricula. More importantly, they must be planted in the minds and hearts of the missions faculty and the students entrusted to them.

1. Spiritual Formation

Ideally, each new believer should be discipled. Discipling involves a disciple who by word and example demonstrates how the biblically normal, constantly growing Christian life should be lived. This demonstration will include daily Bible study, meditation, worship, prayer. It will involve local church membership, personal evangelism and a responsibility to reach out with the gospel. A prospective missionary should be one who has been discipled and who, in turn, is a discipler. Ideally, the discipling of the prospective missionary should have taken place prior to the start of academic training. His or her local church should see that it takes place.

Spiritual formation is a continuing, lifetime process. But several aspects related to preparation for missionary service are extremely important. Foremost among them is the continuing development of a deep devotional life. The prospective missionary must spend quality time with the Lord, meeting Him daily in Bible study, meditation and prayer. People who have spent their lives actively involved in a local church and its programs may be existing on a "spoon-fed" diet of second-hand spiritual food. They have not realized the necessity, on a daily basis, of drawing personal nourishment from the Word.

In North America, such people may survive. But put them in a totally foreign setting with no church, no Bible study, no prayer meeting, nothing in their own language, and they likely will not survive. So missionary preparation must involve this all-important dimension of spiritual formation. As much as possible, college graduates should be growing Christians, evidencing spiritual fruit in their lives.

Regrettably, many students entering college today have never been discipled. Many have not developed good devotional habits. So educators must make provision for the discipling of the potential missionary "disciple-makers." Educators must monitor the devotional lives of their students to be sure this vital area of the Christian life is not neglected.

Spiritual formation, in the sense I am using it, must also include training in spiritual warfare. The Bible has much to say about the subject. Basic passages such as Ephesians 6 outline the weapons of our warfare. Missionaries need to know that they are entering strongholds of satanic power. Satan does not easily give up his hold on the lives of people. Dealing maturely as a cross-cultural worker with spiritual warfare and power encounters must be an essential ingredient in missionary preparation.

2. Emotional Formation

Missionary preparation also involves the emotional life. In this day more often than not, even Christian students coming to a Bible college or seminary have suffered psychological hurt and pain. Many are from homes where parents have been divorced. Many have suffered abuse of various kinds.

Although the needs these people have are best dealt with on the level of the local church fellowship, they often surface when the young person is in college. Interaction with peers and faculty and the added pressures of college life can cause suppressed or hidden emotions to surface. To disregard this aspect of preparation is to overlook a vital area of the prospective missionary's life. Counseling by trained faculty, deans, pastoral staff and professional Christian counselors is an essential part of today's academic preparation for missionaries.

If such problems are not resolved prior to the person's being sent out, they inevitably will cause serious problems, often damaging others as well as the individual. Working in a second language and culture, living with fewer amenities, associating with a very limited number of fellow missionaries increase these tensions. For these reasons and more, there are breakdowns in interpersonal relationships that disrupt field ministries and cause missionaries to return home. Holistic missionary preparation needs to include the opportunity for psychological healing as well as the development of skills in managing conflict.

3. Biblical and Theological Formation

Thorough preparation in biblical and theological studies has always been a major component of academic preparation for missionaries. People who have graduated from Bible college or from seminary are assumed to be competent in these areas. Such assumptions, however, may not always be justified. It is not enough to store cognitive knowledge and be able to quote passage and reference. There must also be an integration of this knowledge into the student's life. That is much more difficult to test in an academic setting.

One of the requirements for missions graduates of the Bible college where I teach is a "senior oral interview." A major component of that interview is a review of the ways in which the graduating senior has incorporated biblical truth into his or her own life.

At times we find a "great gulf fixed" between what the person knows and what is lived out on a daily basis. Of course, the demands of the Western educational process tend to move people along through class after class. There is little time to *integrate* knowledge with real life. Even a substantial number of courses in Bible and theology do not give some individuals a good grasp of Bible knowledge. Care in this area is of utmost importance in the preparation of cross-cultural Christian workers.

Missionaries need to go beyond Western categories of understanding to exegete the Scriptures. They need to be able to apply new insights in the context of the new culture. We need to teach them a Christian response to Islam, folk religions, secularism and various other structures. Ancestor worship, polygamy, spiritism, poverty may not confront the average North American. But they could well confront the missionary. Cognitive knowledge alone will not be adequate. There must be an application of learning in the cross-cultural setting. Missionaries will be living and working in contexts where "doing theology" is a part of their ministry. Academic preparation for this important dimension of the Christian apologetic in the non-Christian world is essential.

4. Cross-Cultural and Missiological Formation

Every prospective missionary today must be well versed in the cross-cultural differences and similarities he or she will face. Each missionary must be equipped with strategies for living and working in a very different culture. The apostle Paul, like Jesus Himself, became part of the group he sought to win in order to be correctly understood by them. Paul became a Jew to the Jews, a Gentile to the Gentiles, weak to the weak. He became "all things to all men so that by all possible means [he] might save some" (1 Corinthians 9:22). Missionary candidates must be prepared to live and work in cultures very different from their own. There are differences, for example, in worldviews, systems of belief, values, modes of thinking, language. There are differences in non-verbal communication, kinship structures and decision-making styles. These are just a few of the cultural models that must be learned in the classroom and applied in field internships. Actual short-term missionary service in cross-cultural internships is now required in some Bible colleges. It must become a standard part of pre-field preparation.

Obviously, missionary training will offer courses

in history of missions, world religions, Bible, theology, counseling. But there is more! The social sciences, particularly cultural anthropology, have given missions a great tool for the communication of the gospel to people in other cultures. Early missionaries went out to diverse cultural groups with little more than a Bible, a toothbrush and a change of clothes! Yet many did great exploits for God, impacting positively on the people among whom they ministered. At the same time, many unknowingly carried with them the cultural baggage of Western civilization. The Christianity they communicated was often a Western form that ultimately isolated the converts from their cultural context. It effectively removed them from meaningful communication with their own people. They lost the cutting edge of evangelism. Christianity became a "foreign" religion, and those who became Christians often became foreigners to their own culture.

Today potential missionaries are trained to understand cultural differences. The evaluation of one's own culture, with its strengths and weaknesses, is an important beginning. With that knowledge the student can develop paradigms to study and understand people in other cultures. Kinship, social structure, political organization, ideology and economics are dynamic forces. They move and control the actions of people. Cultural anthropology offers the missionary analytical tools to understand these systems so different from his or her own. Observation, participant-observation and interviewing are three of these research techniques which help the prospective missionary function knowledgeably in a new culture.

Language of course is a central component of culture. The academic institution must provide the student missionary with an understanding of how to learn a language. He or she may later learn a new language in a structured school setting. He or she may learn the language without the aid of a formal school. The new missionary may even need to develop his or her own language learning program. It is a truism: Language competency is a major factor in any missionary's ultimate success or failure. To learn the language well is a lifetime pursuit. How to learn a language obviously is an essential ingredient in a missionary's academic preparation.

Technology to the Rescue

The missionary who began work even a decade ago would be amazed at the technological advances in training tomorrow's missionaries. In the "information age" in which we are living, the Internet and World Wide Web give us immediate access to research data. At our fingertips, for example, is knowledge concerning unreached people groups the world over. Today's missionary, trained in disciplines unknown to his or her predecessors, should be a far more effective communicator of the gospel.

Those of us who are faculty members and former missionaries often say, "If only we could have had the training young people are getting today." We are sure we would have been more effective, making fewer mistakes, bringing in a greater harvest. Perhaps so. We know that we, as our pioneer predecessors, did the best we could, and God used what we had. Our prayer is that today's academic training will enable tomorrow's missionaries to be even more effective.

Christian cross-cultural training has been going on for almost 2,000 years. Jesus spent three years training a dozen men. Aside from one failure, those whom He trained left us with great examples. Our Lord gave us timeless patterns and principles which we can follow in training others for cross-cultural ministry. The Acts offers word pictures of missionaries struggling with cultural and theological differences. We see the Holy Spirit consistently working to challenge their prejudgments.

I thank God that we, the missions faculty of Bible colleges, graduate schools and seminaries, can participate in the continuing process. May the Lord of the harvest guide and empower us who teach and those whom we train.

There are an estimated 10,000 yet unreached people groups in our world. They can only be reached through a *cross-cultural proclamation* of the good news. I have confidence that our missionary God will lead us onward. Jesus said, "This gospel of the kingdom will be preached in the whole world as a testimony to all nations, and then the end will come" (Matthew 24:14).

Then our King will return. *Then* our missionary task will be finished.

CHAPTER 18

Missions and the Faith Promise

by David C. Thompson

THE FIRST TIME THE LEADERS OF THE Bongolo, Gabon, church heard about the faith promise, they were enthusiastic. They had not found a way to finance their ambitious plans to reach out to other tribes in their area. Appeals to the congregation to give more seemed to fall on deaf ears. The idea of each individual or family making a year-long financial commitment sounded great.

The faith promise is a biblical means to raise money for missionary evangelism. The surrounding tribes needed to hear the good news. To reach them, the people sitting on the straight-backed benches would have to exercise as much faith as their leaders.

The pastors decided I should be the one to explain the system to the congregation. Supposing they had chosen me because of my proven ability to expound deep biblical concepts, I not so modestly agreed to the assignment. The church was having a week-long missionary conference. I chose the opening Sunday to present the faith promise concept.

First I asked the ushers to distribute the small

mimeographed forms I had laboriously prepared the night before. Each said (in rough translation), "With God's help, I promise to give $_____ to the church each month to take the gospel to the unreached." There was also place for a signature.

As the slips of paper were passed down the tightly-packed rows, 400 voices began to murmur in perplexity. The pastor sitting behind me reached for his little bell and rang it vigorously. Slowly the crowd quieted to listen to what I would tell them.

I Explain the Faith Promise

"The faith promise is a promise to God," I said in French. A layman translated my French into Yinzebi so the village mamas and papas in the audience would miss nothing important. So far, everyone seemed happy.

"God asks us through His Word to give some of our money for the work of the church. Abraham, Isaac and Jacob gave a tenth of all they had to God. Their descendants were instructed through Moses to do the same thing."

I sensed a perceptible dulling of interest. The clouds had parted, and the sun poured its rays upon the church's tin roof in uninterrupted blessing. Even the breeze stopped to listen. Sweat dripped off my chin onto the little promise paper in my hand, smearing the ink. I continued with what enthusiasm I could muster.

"When Jesus came to earth, He told people they were to be careful to give a tenth of what they earned to God. But they were not to neglect the other important matters of God's law." I reminded them that God loves a cheerful giver. I explained that God had established the principle of tithing so there would be plenty of money for God's work. Money to support pastors, money to support the Bible school, money to cover the church's other expenses. Then I dropped the bombshell.

"God wants to give you money to give back to Him!" I declared emphatically. The reaction? Complete silence. Were they stunned or just bewildered? I wiped my face with my handkerchief to protect my papers and plowed on. I opened my Bible to Second Corinthians: "God is able to make all grace abound to you, so that in all things at all times, having all that you need, you will abound in every good work. . . . You will be made rich in every way so that you can be generous on every occasion" (9:8, 11).

I Field Their Questions

The translator finished restating what he thought I had said. Then I asked the people to write down how much they wanted God to give them each month to give back to him for missions. Since it was a promise, I asked them to sign their names.

An older man who irritated me to no end because of his wishy-washy faith had a question. "What if when the time comes, we don't have the money?" I breathed deeply and explained that no one who did not pay would be asked for the money. This was a promise to God, not to the church.

"If it's a promise to God, why do we have to sign our names? Why do we even have to turn in this piece of paper to the church?" Gabonese hate to sign their names to anything, because it makes a promise binding. Heads on all sides nodded in agreement, and a low rumble of discussion spread across the congregation. It even infected the gray-haired elders, who sat behind me on the platform for moral support. I began to understand why they had considered me so unusually qualified to explain the faith promise to the congregation!

The pastor rang his bell furiously, and the crowd again quieted.

As sweetly as possible I responded to Mr. Wishy-Washy. "If you don't believe that God can give you the money to give back to Him, don't sign the paper. Don't turn it in to the church." To the whole congregation I continued: "If you have enough faith to believe that God can do this, write in as much money as you think God is good for. Sign your name and put the paper in the offering plate that will be at the door after the service. We will add up the total and announce it to everyone. Then we'll know how much money we'll have to work with each month."

This seemed to go down well, and there were some encouraging nods. Then a dear old saint from the women's side of the church rose rheumatically to her feet.

"What if—" She paused for dramatic effect, then started again. "What if someone can't sign his name or write any numbers?" This time the pastor's bell could not be heard above the amused noise of the congregation. The dear woman sat down in a huff.

When the crowd had quieted, I explained that just a mark somewhere on the paper would indicate each one's sincerity. People could ask someone else to write in the amount they wanted to give each month. God would understand what was in their hearts.

We Were Off to a Rocky Start

Not all went smoothly with the faith promise. For starters, the ushers forgot to put an offering plate at the door, so most people took their little slips of paper home. The next Sunday, the ushers again forgot to put out an offering plate. It didn't matter. Most members had forgotten to bring their faith promises. Two weeks after my presentation, we had in hand fewer than 20 faith promises.

But the following week the ushers remembered and the people remembered. We ended up with over 200 completed papers. Some had misunderstood and written in not a monthly figure but a figure for the entire year. And a few thought it was to be a one-time offering rather than a month by month promise.

Still, when the first month's receipts were tallied, the missions offering totalled over $200. And that from a church with a greater than 50 percent unemployment rate.

About every other month, the church leaders forgot to receive the missions offering. Many simply took their gifts to the pastor, and he (to his credit) passed them on to the treasurer. Despite the initial confusion, the people had come to understand the principle of faith-giving. Intuitively they knew that it pleased God.

With these funds, the church leaders were able to make regular trips to preach to two unreached tribal groups in their district. Over the next two years, they established six churches. On two occasions they invited men and women with leadership potential from these new churches to come to

Bongolo for a short-term Bible school. In this way the local church people were able to see some of the fruit of their giving.

The Faith Promise Is About Faith

The faith promise is about faith. Jesus, who blessed and multiplied five loaves of bread and a few fish to feed 5,000 people, is still living. He is still powerful. He is still with us. He wants to entrust us with all the money we dare ask Him for to carry out His work. How much do we believe He can give us in a month or a year for this purpose?

Jesus explained to His disciples how He would respond to believers' needs. One of His clearest teachings came in response to two blind men who asked Jesus to heal them.

> [Jesus] asked them, "Do you believe that I am able to do this?"
> "Yes, Lord," they replied.
> Then he touched their eyes and said, "According to your faith will it be done to you"; and their sight was restored. (Matthew 9:28-30)

Do you see it? Do you believe that Jesus is able to give you what you want to give for missions? His answer is this: "According to your faith will it be done to you." Ask for $1,000, or $10,000 or even $1 million. I do not have the slightest doubt that if your motives are pure and you sincerely believe that God is able to do it, He will do it. Many of us, however, are afraid that God will fail. To protect God (or is it to protect ourselves?), we shrink back from putting our faith to the test.

"We're So Broke We Can't Give"

A few years ago I was speaking at a church in the Midwest. The local economy was in a slump, good jobs were scarce and many of the church families were struggling to make ends meet. I had preached several times, challenging the members to make missions a priority in their lives. After one such sermon, a young couple waited for me at I greeted people at the door.

The husband and wife were relatively young, and as they waited, their two small children fussed impatiently. Finally all the others had gone and we were alone. As they came up to me and introduced themselves, I noticed there were tears in their eyes. The wife, who was dressed in clean but faded jeans, a sweatshirt and scuffed tennis shoes, spoke first.

"Dr. Thompson, we were really touched by your message. More than anything, we'd like to do something to help. But how can we? My husband is between jobs, we have two small children, and we are unable even to pay all of our bills."

At that point the husband, dressed as plainly as his wife, spoke up. "We'd like to give for missions," he agreed, "but we're so broke we can't even give regularly to this church."

Then and there I explained to them the principle of faith giving. They didn't have to have money. They just had to have faith that God could give them money to give back to Him. This clearly was a new idea to them.

When I had finished explaining, I asked them what they thought. Both of them looked doubtful.

"How much money are we talking about?" the young man asked nervously.

"How much do you think God can give you in a year from 'out of the blue' to give to missions?" I asked in reply. The man glanced at his wife and shrugged. She raised her eyebrows and shook her head. It was clear she didn't have a clue as to what to propose.

"How About $500?"

"Do you think God can give you $1,000 this year to give for missions?" I pressed. They looked at each other for a long moment without speaking. I could see that they didn't think God could give them that much.

"How about $500?" I countered. After a moment, the husband suggested $600.

"But what if we can't pay it?" he asked.

"I'm not talking about money that you're counting on earning to live on," I replied. "I'm talking about money you weren't expecting—money 'out of the blue.' Do you believe that God can give you $600 like that?"

After another moment of hesitation, the wife responded. "We're willing to try! But I don't see how we can do it. I don't see where the money can come from. We don't have rich relatives, and we don't stand to inherit anything from our parents." I assured her that it would be no problem for God to come up with the money. The problem might be that when God provided the money they had asked for, they might spend the money on themselves.

Both of them indignantly declared they would never do such a thing. But I gently explained that many people who make faith promises do just that with their windfall. To help build their faith and remember their promise, I encouraged them to fill out a faith promise card. Unlike the papers we used in Bongolo, Gabon, these cards were printed on thick, glossy paper in three colors with ink that would not run when moist.

While I waited, the husband filled out a card, writing in the amount of $600 on both parts of the card. One part he kept; the other part he turned into the church office. Before I left, I prayed for them, asking God to honor their faith.

"Write to me when the money comes in," I urged. "I want to know how God has provided!" They laughed to cover up their doubt, but they did promise to write.

About six months later, I received a letter from the Midwest. In the busyness of preparing to return to Africa for another four years, I had completely forgotten my conversation with the couple.

"You'll Never Believe What Happened!"

"Dear Dr. Thompson," the letter began, "You'll never believe what happened!" It was the young wife who was writing. As I read on, she described how several months after the missionary conference she and her husband were involved in a serious automobile accident. Although they and their children were not hurt, their only car was very badly damaged. It was insured, so they followed the insurer's instructions. Even before I reached the end of the letter, I knew its outcome. The details were involved, but the insurance settlement turned out to be $600 more than the actual repair costs!

The husband and wife were thrilled by God's response to their step of faith. So thrilled, in fact, that they were making another faith promise for missions for the rest of the year! I have no doubt that God has continued to respond to their faith. And to provide as well for their own family needs.

I have that assurance because of the vivid picture God paints through the prophet Malachi. God complains that His people are robbing Him by withholding not only their tithes but also their offerings. He challenges them to test Him by obedience.

> *"Test me in this," says the* LORD *Almighty, "and see if I will not throw open the floodgates of heaven and pour out so much blessing that you will not have room enough for it. I will prevent pests from devouring your crops, and the vines in your fields will not cast their fruit."*
>
> (Malachi 3:10-11)

God Is Waiting to Bless Us

Imagine God in heaven looking with disappointment at an enormous pile of goods. It is atop a huge trapdoor, and one of His angels holds a cord attached to the latch. The angel looks hopefully at God, awaiting the signal to open the trapdoor. But God only shakes His head. Why won't God let the angel open the door and let the goods fall to His people? Why won't God bless His people materially?

I used to think it was because God knows that abundant material blessings can draw us away from dependency on Him. But that is not the reason God cites through Malachi. The real problem is that God's people don't believe He can provide enough for them to live on. No matter how much or how little they have, they think they can't *afford* to tithe and give appropriate offerings to God. As long as they hold onto what God asks them to give, God withholds what He would like to give them. *God's people are disobedient in their giving because their faith is untested and weak!*

It is an established fact that evangelical Christians in North America have a higher standard of living than did either their grandparents or their parents. They have more material blessings. Rarely, if ever, do they experience hunger. They enjoy better health, increasing amounts of recreation, more opportunities.

Yet these same Christians give a smaller percentage of what they earn and own to the cause of Christ. At a time when Christians have more material resources than they ever have had, how is it that missions budgets remain static or even shrink? The answer is very simple. *Christians have forgotten how to live and to give by faith.* They hold ever more tightly to their shrinking supply of expendable cash. And God shakes his head at the hopeful angel holding the cord to the trapdoor latch of heaven's blessings. The less God's people give back to Him in faith, the less God gives them to give. That's the simple message of Malachi 3:10-11.

Do Our Present Offerings Please God?

This raises a question about the act of giving. Does our present giving bring any pleasure to God? Earlier God says to His people through the same prophet Malachi, "I will accept no offering from your hands" (1:10). Why? Because of their attitude. The people were making offerings—of sorts—but they were saying to themselves, "What a burden!"

(1:12-13). They were offering God their crippled and diseased animals (1:8). God says:

> When you bring injured, crippled or diseased animals and offer them as sacrifices, should I accept them from your hands? . . . Cursed is the cheat who has an acceptable male in his flock and vows to give it, but then sacrifices a blemished animal to the Lord. For I am a great king, . . . and my name is to be feared among the nations. (1:13-14)

How can we please God in our giving? Many of us have memorized the answer to that question. We carry it around in our heads without even understanding what it means. "Without faith it is impossible to please God, because anyone who comes to him must believe that he exists and that he rewards those who earnestly seek him" (Hebrews 11:6).

We must give to God by faith, not by what we know we have in our bank accounts. That is the essence of the faith promise.

In 1995 the Bongolo church was so busy with other projects that it didn't get around to planning a missionary conference. In spite of that, some of the people who had made faith promises the previous year continued each month to give what they had promised. Among them was the old mama who had to ask one of her grandchildren to write down the amount she wished to give.

In November thieves broke into the church office and stole the church's money. Included was some $500 in the missions account. The theft forcefully reminded the church leaders that if their mission work was to continue, they needed to plan another missionary conference.

At the conference, held in March, 1996, people were again challenged to make a faith promise. This time, they needed less convincing. Many had already seen God provide the money they had promised to give. After the first week, with about three-quarters of the faith promises collected, the total stood at $200 a month. And this from Christians who earn between $40 and $200 a month. And who support their church and pastor besides.

Already, the church leaders are planning where to go next with the good news of Jesus.

Missions and the Missionaries' Kids

CHAPTER	
19	

by J. Evan Evans

SOME OF THE BIGGEST LESSONS I'VE ever learned about prayer were taught to me by junior highers at an "MK" school. My wife, Jewel, and I were dorm parents to 9 of them (plus 19 other kids) at the International Christian Academy in Bouaké, Côte d'Ivoire, West Africa.

All of it started at a time when I was struggling with my own prayer life. I prayed, but my prayers were stale. Not much seemed to be happening. Then I came across Wesley L. Duewel's book, *Touch the World through Prayer*. It began to revolutionize my praying. So I, in turn, decided to share what God was teaching me with my junior high kids during dorm devotions.

As devotions concluded that evening, Jonathan handed me a note.

"Wait until I'm down the hall before you read it," he requested mysteriously. (Thirteen-year-old boys get easily embarrassed.) So I waited, and then I read it:

Dear Uncle Evan,

I haven't been in the habit of praying much lately, but after I heard your devotional tonight on the subject of prayer, I feel like praying my heart out tonight!

The next evening I had two books that I was thinking of using for devotions with the kids. One was an exciting book about God's miracles. And of course the other book was *Touch the World through Prayer*. I asked the kids which they preferred. Jonathan spoke up.

"I want to hear more about prayer!" he said emphatically. I wasn't sure how the other kids felt. But junior high peer pressure is a marvelous thing. One by one, the others nodded. "Yeah, let's hear more about prayer."

Praying in Jesus' Name

That evening, I shared about the power that we have in the name of Jesus. So often the phrase, "in Jesus' name, Amen" is just an ending that we slap on the end of our prayers to let people know we are finished. But it is *the name of Jesus* that gives our prayers power and validity! One of the last things Jesus did before He went to heaven was to teach the disciples to pray in His name.

After sharing this with the kids, I told them that we weren't going to go through the usual prayer routine. Until then, it had consisted of a few standard requests: "Dear Heavenly Father, Thank you for this day. Please help us to get A's on our tests tomorrow. Help us to win the soccer game. And please give us *x, y* and *z*. I told them that instead, they were to pray as God led them.

Prayer time was going reasonably well. But the turning point came when Osman began to pray. Osman, one of our international students who had not been reared in a Christian home, was unfamiliar with all the spiritual "jargon." He had found the Lord while a student at the Academy. It was refreshing to hear Osman pray because he prayed from the heart. He didn't rely on the usual clichés that many of us use. For example, one time Osman prayed, "Lord, sometimes people look at me and say I'm a 'holy roller.' But, to be honest with You—and I don't mean to be rude, Lord—I really don't give a rip."

On this particular night, Osman seemed to sense an oppression while we were praying. In the middle of his prayer, he suddenly paused.

"Excuse me, Lord, but I have a few things to say to Satan." I wondered what in the world he was going to say to Satan! Osman continued:

"Satan, you are a defeated foe. Jesus Christ defeated you at the cross. We are God's children, covered by the blood of Jesus, and you have no right being here. And so, in the name of Jesus, I command you to get out of here!"

One of the other boys testified that he had been carrying a burden that night. At that exact moment, he felt the burden lift. Another boy said that while his head was bowed and his eyes were closed, at the exact moment of Osman's prayer he saw a flash of bright light. Everyone sensed the unrestricted presence of the Holy Spirit. All the kids started praying like they had never prayed before.

"Lord, I Need You More than Anybody!"

"Lord," Jon Marc prayed, "we always pray for

other people that need You." Then he broke down and began to weep. "Lord," he continued, "I need you more than anybody! Please come and fill me."

Prayer time went on for nearly two hours. After I closed, heads popped up and I could see the excitement written all over the kids' faces.

"Uncle Evan," one of the fellows said, "I can't explain what a wonderful experience that was. That was better than scoring the winning goal in the World Cup soccer finals!" For a boy raised in West Africa, scoring in World Cup soccer was the ultimate of thrills! The kids were really wound up. All they could talk about was how awesome it was to experience the presence of God like that. Once one of the girls tried to change the subject, but a boy said, "No, we don't want to talk about that. We want to talk about the glory of the Lord!"

When 11 o'clock came, I told the kids they needed to get some sleep. They all had school the next day. I promised to pick up the next evening where we had left off. They all cooperated and went to bed—or so I thought. I learned afterwards that the boys were too excited to sleep. They ended up in the bathroom, sitting on the cold floor. Shawn had the Bible in which his mother had highlighted some key verses. He went through it, page by page, reading the key verses out loud to the other boys. There were exclamations such as "Wow! That's a good one!" Every now and then someone suggested, "Let's sing . . ." Or, "Let's pray!" And after they had sung or prayed (quietly), "OK, now read another verse, Shawn!" They sat on that bathroom floor singing, praying and reading Scripture until 2 in the morning!

On their way out the door to school the next day,

they turned around, shook their fists at me and shouted, "Praise the Lord!"

In all honesty, I wondered if this was a one-night spiritual high. But it did not prove to be so. That evening, there was the same excitement. Prayer time went for two hours. At one point, one of the boys said they needed to tell the rest of the campus about what God was doing in their lives.

"Wait Until They Ask"

"No," countered another fellow wisely. "We need to wait until they see that God is doing something in our lives. Then when they ask, we'll tell them all about it. But they need to see a difference in us first."

Others *did* begin to notice a difference in these kids. Teachers began to ask us what was happening with them. One teacher said that Shem had stood up at the beginning of her Bible class and challenged all the students:

"This is not English. This is not history. This is *Bible* class. This is *the Word of God!* It is the most important thing we can ever study. We need to take this seriously and learn from it."

We noticed that the kids were beginning to hold each other accountable for their words and actions. One day my wife happened to overhear two of the boys talking down the hall.

"I heard what you said to Joe today at the soccer game. I don't mean to get on your case or anything, but do you think that was pleasing to God?"

There was a pause, and then the other boy answered. "No, you're right. I need to go and apologize." Never in all our years of working with youth had we seen anything like this. Jewel and I marveled over this type of accountability, especially among junior high kids.

The "revival" went on for five weeks, and then Easter vacation came. The students were to go home for a two-week break, and I wondered if their enthusiasm for God and prayer would continue when they returned. When the kids returned from vacation, they picked up where they had left off. In fact, they asked if they could also begin getting up earlier in the mornings to *begin* their day with prayer together.

One weekend, I took the six boys out to a rock quarry a few miles from the campus for an overnight camp out. We had a good time climbing rocks, talking, hunting frogs and of course praying. Just before we broke camp the next morning, we sat up on the rocks overlooking the water below, taking in the African scenery all around us. We were having a time of prayer together, and as usual the Spirit of God was evident. One of the boys was asking the Holy Spirit "to sweep over us like a mighty, rushing wind." At that precise moment, we all heard and felt a powerful gust of wind that came blowing through the rock quarry. It gave us goosebumps!

The Prayer Revival Spreads

Earlier in the school year, I had been asked to speak at the five-day senior class retreat. With what was happening in the lives of the junior-highers in our dorm, I decided to change my topic to the subject of prayer. I shared with the seniors what God was teaching our junior high kids about prayer. I told how it was transforming their lives.

The seniors returned to the school excited about prayer. They wanted to know if they could meet with the junior high kids for prayer. I announced this request in our dorm, assuming the kids' response would be a definite yes. I knew how much they looked up to and respected the seniors. But my kids surprised me by saying, "No, not yet." They explained that if the seniors met with them for prayer, they might pray to impress the seniors rather than to focus on worshiping God.

Finally, after some time had passed, the junior highers said they were ready to invite the seniors for a time of prayer. Three senior fellows comprised the first group to come. They shared what God was teaching *them* about prayer and then led our junior high kids in a time of prayer. Afterward, the three seniors came to me.

"Uncle Evan, thanks so much for allowing us to come and pray with your kids. We came thinking we would show them what prayer was all about, but we were totally blown away! What an awesome experience it was to listen to those kids pray!"

Before this prayer revival, I once had talked to the junior high kids about how they could bring revival to the whole school campus. At the time, they couldn't fathom how God could use little junior-highers in that way. After all, they were so young. What high schooler (let alone adult) would listen to them?

Now that they had experienced God in such a real way, I again challenged them to be God's tools of revival to the whole campus. This time, they weren't so skeptical. I asked them if they would be willing to visit some of the high school dorms during devotions and share what God was teaching them. Their response: "We are willing to share. God can do the rest."

One evening, Jewel took three of the boys to one of the girls' dorms for devotions. When they first walked into the dorm and faced those 20 high school girls, they had a moment of panic. They asked my wife if they could first go into a back room and pray. During that prayer time, they asked God to speak to "every single girl's heart." They asked that not one girl would leave that night without being touched by God. Jewel then took them to the lounge for the devotional time.

The three boys began to share with the girls what God had been teaching them about prayer. They were a bit nervous, but when prayer time came, they instantly were at ease and bold. It was obvious that the girls were not used to spending much time in prayer during dorm devotions.

"I Want to Know You Like They Know You!"

All three boys prayed. Then one of the girls prayed. Then Jewel prayed. The girls seemed to assume that the prayer time was over. But then our three boys prayed again. And Jewel prayed again. And each of the three boys prayed again. An hour or so passed, the girls all this time listening to the three boys praying so fervently. Finally, one girl broke down crying.

"Lord," she prayed, "after sitting here listening to these boys pray, I realize that *I don't know You like I should!* I want to know You like they know You, Lord!" (What made the scene especially poignant was that one of the boys was this girl's little brother.)

The girl finished her prayer. Then an incredible thing happened. One by one, the other girls in the room began praying and confessing and crying out to God. When it was over, two hours had passed! As the girls raised their heads, there was not a dry eye in the room! Truly the boys' prayers at the beginning of the evening had been answered.

During those two hours, the rest of our junior high kids were back in our dorm bombarding their buddies with prayer support. What a wonderful reunion they all had as the three fellows returned to report how God had worked! We broke out Cokes and popped popcorn to celebrate all God had done.

A couple of weeks later, I took three different fellows to a high school boys' dorm. Once again God worked through in a phenomenal way. One of the high school boys came to me after it was over and said he felt like he had just gone fifteen rounds with the world champion boxer! He said that each time one of our boys would confess a weakness to the Lord, he would end up saying, "Yes, that's me too, Lord!" This happened so many times that he felt really worked over by the Lord. But he said he was thankful because it was something he really needed.

A missionary from Mali who was visiting the school asked if she might sit in on our dorm devotions. As usual, our kids prayed for about two hours.

"That was such a blessing!" the missionary commented to me afterwards. "There are saints in Mali who don't pray like that!"

One evening I was walking around the campus and a high school girl approached me.

"Uncle Evan, could I come and have devotions with your junior high kids tonight? I really need a touch from the Lord."

The Spirit of God Was Present

Why would a high school girl want to have a time of prayer with junior high kids? Why would a missionary from Mali be so blessed by prayer time with these kids? Why would a whole dorm of high school girls be so moved by the prayers of three young boys? Why were three high school boys "blown away" after listening to these kids pray?

The answer is simple. When these kids began to pray, it was evident that the Holy Spirit was present. They could—and did—pray for two hours without even realizing how much time had passed. In fact, there were times when I closed off the prayer time after two hours and the boys asked, "Why so soon?"

Their prayers focused on three major areas: praise and worship, the Scriptures and confession.

The major part of the prayer time was spent in worship of God. They referred to His qualities of character by using His Hebrew names. They thanked Him for His many attributes. They learned not to be thinking of what they would say when their turn came. Rather, they listened well while the other person was praying and fed off of each other's thoughts, praying with one mind. They allowed the Holy Spirit to direct their praise. Sometimes one of them would lead out in a worship chorus and the others would join in.

Once while we were praying, one of the boys said, "Lord, as I sit here, I am struck by Your awesomeness. I can no longer just sit here." Immediately he fell to his knees before the Lord. One by one, the others knelt as well.

The more the kids grew in the Lord, the more

time they spent in the Scriptures. They began to realize the power of the Word. As they keyed off of each other's thoughts, they would quote Scripture. They recited verses of praise. They reminded the Lord of what He had promised in His Word. They encouraged each other by quoting Bible passages.

Sometimes they referred to Scripture passages (such as verses about authority) that God used to convict others in the group. They also quoted Bible verses having to do with spiritual warfare. Boldly they took the offensive in spiritual battle as they stood on the truth of God's Word.

On many occasions, under the intense, felt presence of the Holy Spirit, there was confession of sin. If one of them was struggling with some issue, it was difficult for him to sit there for long without feeling convicted. Invariably, confession followed. This confession came as a result of a healthy concept of a loving Father, not a harsh, vindictive God. One time Shem confessed, "Lord, today I heard Your voice speaking to me, and I ignored You. I realize how much You love me, and I don't want to grieve You by my disobedience. Please forgive me!"

A Vision Expanded

The exciting thing about this prayer revival among our junior high kids was that it lasted until the end of the school year. Fifteen whole weeks! As the school year came to a close, we realized that only a few of those kids would be returning the next year. The rest would be with furloughing parents in their homelands or leaving Côte d'Ivoire for good. Soon the group would be dispersed around the world.

Just before they all left, we got up at 5 a.m. for our final prayer time together. We went out to the rock quarry once again and sat on the rocks overlooking the water below us.

On one hand we were sad. We knew we would all be going in different directions. On the other hand, we were able to marvel at how God had used a seemingly insignificant group of young kids to touch a missions-sponsored boarding school through prayer.

Now it was time to go out, to expand our vision. It was time to touch the *world* through prayer!

<table>
<tr><td>

CHAPTER

20

</td><td>

Missions and Miracles

by Jean A. Livingston

</td></tr>
</table>

SEVERAL HUNDRED NOISY, BANDAGED YOUNG men sat before us in the auditorium of the Cong Hoa military hospital in Saigon. All of them were wearing loose-fitting, faded blue pajamas. All of them were South Vietnamese soldiers, wounded while defending their country from the Communists. Some—with badly maimed bodies—would be discharged. Most would mend and return to the battle zones.

Betty Hunt and I were non-Vietnamese civilians—North American missionaries. But God, in His great mercy, had opened a wide and effective door of evangelism to the South Vietnamese military. Not the least was these Sunday evening gospel rallies at Cong Hoa (KOM Wah).

Our husbands, Garth Hunt and Jim Livingston, together with other missionaries, had helped haul the more seriously injured to the auditorium. There would be a sports film (the drawing card), singing, an appropriate message from God's Word and, at the end, an invitation to repent and follow Christ. We had committed every part of the rally to the Lord.

But certainly we had not anticipated the mass invasion of flying termites on this night.

The Vietnamese welcome the coming of the termites. They mark the imminent break in the torrid heat and the coming of welcomed rain. The pattern is always the same. The long-winged creatures emerge from the ground by the billions, take to the air, find mates and die. During their brief sojourn above ground, they are attracted to lights. No place is off limits to their assault. The only escape is to turn off the lights and go to bed! By morning, all that remains are detached wings and dead termites.

But we were in the midst of an evangelistic service at Cong Hoa hospital. Young men were in that audience who desperately needed Jesus. Already we could see that the soldiers were being distracted by these aggravating insects. The guest speaker was finding it difficult to bat bugs and preach at the same time.

I do not know how Betty prayed, and she could not hear my own silent prayer. But both of us brought the matter before our Lord. Then we turned our attention again to the speaker. Perhaps five minutes passed. I noticed that the men seemed held in rapt attention by the speaker's message. Then I looked all around the auditorium.

"Betty!" I whispered. "It's incredible! The flying termites are gone!"

Betty and I expected the intervention of God, and He had not disappointed us. Absolutely contrary to nature, those millions of termites in the auditorium were gone. That evening, at the invitation, some 35 Vietnamese soldiers turned their lives over to Jesus Christ.

Signs and Wonders Accompanied the Gospel in Vietnam

The history of the church in Vietnam is generously sprinkled with stories of the supernatural. In the pioneer days, new believers expected God's intervention. And it happened, not because of the faith of the missionaries but because of the faith of new believers. They were convinced that God's power was greater than the power of the evil spirits. Hundreds of people were first attracted to the *Tin Lanh* church because they saw these unusual evidences of God's power and presence.

Our analytical minds are prone to ask: *What are the components of a miracle?* The response comes as quickly: *Who knows?* One thing is certain: God is sovereign and He is in control. We missionaries to Vietnam have witnessed, either personally or through the eyes of national Christians, quiet miracles. They have brought glory to the name of the Lord Jesus.

We discovered two principles: First, *miracles are God-initiated.* We pray and pray fervently, but we dare not tell God how to do His work. He determines the manner in which He will act. Second, *our part is simply to obey His Word.*

A pastor who worked with us in military evangelism had a college-age daughter, whom I will call Mai (MY)—not her real name. Mai was suffering from an obstruction which the doctor insisted needed immediate surgery. Another missionary, concerned about Mai, approached me with a suggestion. If we were in unity of spirit and believed healing was God's will for Mai, we should visit her.

Specifically, we should lay hands on this girl and pray for her healing. Convinced that the prompting was from the Lord, the two of us set out the following afternoon.

Thus we believed our visit to Mai's home was God-initiated. Our part was simply to obey the inner prompting of God's Spirit. What happened after that would be in God's hands.

To our surprise, the entire family—mother, father and several adult children—were gathered in the small living room awaiting our arrival. We stated the purpose of our visit.

"But before we pray," my missionaey friend interjected, "Mrs. Livingston will read from James 5."

I opened my Vietnamese Bible and read,

> *Is any one of you in trouble? . . . Is any one of you sick? He should call the elders of the church to pray over him and anoint him with oil in the name of the Lord. And the prayer offered in faith will make the sick person well; the Lord will raise him up. If he has sinned, he will be forgiven. Therefore confess your sins to each other and pray for each other so that you may be healed.* (James 5:13-16)

No sooner had I finished reading than Mai's younger sister stood to her feet and began to weep. This young woman had earned an unfavorable reputation. With strong emotion she wailed, "Oh, Lord, do not let my sin be a hindrance to my sister's healing. I confess and repent right now! Lord, forgive me."

Then, one by one, the rest of the family stood. With heads bowed and hands folded in the polite Vietnamese way, they confessed their sins to God and to one another. After many tears, we were finally ready to anoint Mai with oil. Now we could ask God to heal His child.

A Changed Atmosphere

At the sound of the last *Amen*, the atmosphere in the small parsonage changed from a spirit of heaviness to one of joy. Excitedly, everyone began talking at the same time as to the best way to inform the surgeon of the change in plans. My friend and I just stood by and watched this Vietnamese family council in action. Since surgery was imminent, the family decided that the father-pastor would visit the doctor's office the very next day.

At the doctor's office, when the pastor gently requested another X-ray, the doctor was uncharacteristically angry. He banged the fist on the table. Insinuating that the pastor was ungrateful, he stomped out of the office.

The surgeon's anger and lack of self-control was further evidence to the pastor that God was closing the door to surgery. The pastor came direct from the doctor's office to our house to report this development.

The prayer of faith, the anointing of oil, the confession of sins were the components of the miracle. But without a doubt it was God's power that performed the mighty act. Mai was completely healed of her physical problem. When we saw her the next Sunday, she had completely regained her strength and color. She became a living testimony of God's greatness. Her miraculous healing was the talk of the community. And God was honored and exalted.

Lanh's Personal Miracle

Three large transport buses roar to a stop at the departure sector of the Philippine Refugee Processing Center in Bataan. It is the place where Jim and I have been working more recently, now that we cannot be in Vietnam. Adjoining the departure sector is the Evangelical Chapel serving the refugee center. Sunday morning worship is in progress.

A young Vietnamese man, one of the refugees, gets up from his seat and proceeds to the front of the chapel. Lanh (LAHN) has requested permission to give his testimony this morning. In only one hour he will be leaving the refugee center on one of those three buses. It is appropriate that he express appreciation and say farewell to the Christian community at the center.

Tonight Lanh and the other departing refugees will sleep at the Transit Center in Manila—refugees jokingly call it "Mosquito Bite Hotel." And tomorrow is his special day, the day Lanh has waited for over five years. Tomorrow at last he will fly to *Nuoc My,* "Beautiful Land," the distinct name Vietnamese have always called America.

"Honorable missionaries and brothers and sisters in Christ," Lanh begins, addressing all of us in the church service. He is about to tell us how he came to faith in Christ. "Eight years ago in Vietnam I was taken captive by the communist security police. Although I was not guilty of any crime, they led me off to the prison on the outskirts of Saigon."

Jim and I had learned from other refugees at the processing center that this was a common tactic of the communist government. Anyone who during the war in Vietnam had been in the elite special forces units of the Vietnamese army was a special target. So were Vietnamese who had been involved with Americans. These were arrested and tried—sometimes by force—and "re-educated" in the prison system.

Inhumane Treatment

As Lanh continues, he tells how he was stripped of his clothes, shackled hand and foot, then locked in what he called "a box." For *three and a half months* Lanh suffered in that despicable condition, he tells the congregation. Not once was he untied, not even to eat his meals or to attend to his personal needs. Not once in that time was he allowed out of his torture box.

Of course, the purpose of the torment was to crack the mind and whip the will of the fated prisoner. "At times I wanted to die," Lanh says as he remembers the suffering and indescribable misery.

But thoughts of home and family kept him alive. That and a tiny thing that Lanh calls *duc tin*—faith. Faith in a Being Lanh terms *Duc Chua Troi*, the one Supreme God of the Heavens. Lanh was not then a Christian. At that point he knew nothing of Jesus Christ.

"My faith at that time was exceptionally small," Lanh admits, "but it kept me from becoming insane."

Three and a half months into that inhumane treatment, Lanh was suddenly unshackled and transferred to a more traditional prison cell. It was dark and putrid with the repulsive stench of mold, filth and urine. He would coinhabit the place with an assortment of insect pests and vermin that had preceded him. But wait! There was yet Another.

"Little by little," Lanh continues, "the Supreme God of the Heavens began to reveal Himself to me. I did not understand this, but I could feel His presence with me in my cell. And so I did not hesitate to talk with Him."

A Paper Clip

One day Lanh glanced down near the metal door of his cell. Lying on the floor was an ordinary paper clip. Lanh picked it up. *Who passed down the dark corridor and dropped this little paper clip?* Lanh wondered. Almost instantly, a thought came to his mind: *Open it! Open it!*

Ever so carefully, Lanh pulled the paper clip apart and straightened it. Then he proceeded to reshape the wire into a new form—the form of a key. Satisfied with its shape, Lanh waited until dark to test his creation.

Click! The bolt within the lock slid to the open position. The heavy, metal cell door was no longer locked! Oh, the surge of emotion that filled Lanh's body! His pulse raced. He had been given a way out of his misery!

But Lanh was shaky with alarm. He knew he had the means to escape, but he had no plan. Getting out of his cell was but the beginning. Without a carefully calculated plan, escape was impossible. A bullet to his head would end everything. Carefully Lanh relocked the cell door.

For several days Lanh pondered his situation. Finally he raised his face toward the ceiling and spoke to the Presence. "Show me, Supreme God, what to do. What time would be best to attempt an escape? Please answer me."

Almost at once, an idea came to Lanh's mind. He searched his cell and found a scrap of paper that he quickly tore into five smaller bits. On each he scratched a number: 1, 2, 3, 4, 5—a number for each night hour after midnight. Next, he scrambled the bits of paper and drew one of them. It was the number 2. Two in the morning! *Of course, that would be the perfect hour. Blessed be the Supreme Holy One!*

Lanh lay down on his straw mat confident the Presence would awaken him at the designated hour. The early crowing of a rooster—Asian roosters seem to crow off and on for hours before dawn—awakened him.

Escape!

Noiselessly Lahn inserted his little paper-clip key in the metal door. Would it open a second time? Would his plan to escape succeed? Lanh's heart was pounding with such intensity that he feared the prisoners in nearby cells would be awakened. Gently he turned the delicate wire.

A soft click, and the door opened quietly! Then it was barefeet fleeing down the corridor, past a sleeping guard, out the door. It was a dash across the open courtyard, past another guard deep in sleep. Even a mongrel pup curled up near the guardhouse did not rouse.

Somehow Lanh maneuvered over a fence strung with coils of barbed wire. With all the strength he could muster, he raced through the blackness across an open field to *freedom!*

But Lanh knew that come morning, his escape would be obvious. He was a wanted man now. Even though the simple peasants in the nearby village befriended him, Lanh knew he would have to leave Vietnam at once. Another miracle! The Supreme One made possible his escape from Vietnam by boat.

Another camp. This time it was not a prison camp but a refugee camp in Thailand where thousands of Indo-China's "boat people" were sheltered and given sustenance. Within two days of his arrival, Lanh had a visit from Christians, the *Tin Lanh,* or "Good News" people. They welcomed him and shared the gospel with this new arrival.

Lanh tells us he listened with unusual interest to the story of this *Duc Chua Troi,* the Supreme God of the Heavens who loved people so much that He gave His Son to die as a sacrifice for their sins.

Everything in Focus

Suddenly, Lanh says, everything began to come into focus. This God they were telling him about was the God who had revealed Himself to Lanh in the "box" of physical torture. He was the Presence in his cell who kept his mind secure. It was He who had given Lanh the means to escape. It was He who later kept Lanh's boat safe on the dangerous sea voyage to Thailand.

Suddenly Lanh could see it all clearly! He was jubilant as he realized the God they were speaking of was the God who had been revealing Himself to Lahn.

In that hour Lanh bowed his head and accepted Christ as his Savior and Lord.

As Lanh concludes his testimony at the Philippine Refugee Processing Center, he says apologetically to the Christians: "I just did not know that His Name was Jesus!"

Who can command God and tell Him how to manifest His power? No one. Yet as supernatural creatures, we know there is more to life than what we can comprehend naturally. Jesus tells us to ask in order to receive. The psalmist encourages us to

> *Give thanks to the LORD, call on his name;*
> *make known among the nations what he*
> *has done. . . .*
> *Remember the wonders he has done,*
> *his miracles, and . . .*
> *Praise the LORD.* (Psalm 105: 1, 5, 45)

Missions and Spiritual Warfare

CHAPTER

21

by David O. Manske

EVERY CHURCH-GOER AND SUNDAY SCHOOL student knows the story of David and Goliath. Young David is a timeless example of courage and faith as he faced the formidable Philistine giant.

But another element in the story of David and Goliath has always intrigued me: the Israelite army. Here was a fighting force with a reputation for winning wars. Not that the army itself was so powerful or skilled. But God fought for Israel. When God was on Israel's side, the army was invincible.

Why was this powerful army stalled in its tracks? Why were all its fighting men petrified into inactivity? Young David was eager to confront Goliath. The Israelite army seemed eager to avoid such a confrontation. The army was full of fear. David was full of faith. The army had equipment. David had only his slingshot. But he was ready to use it.

My wife, Susanna, and I arrived here in Brazil in 1989. We were well aware of the pervasive spiritism in this country. As we faced the Brazilian reality, we were somewhat prepared for spiritual warfare. Even so, the eerie shrieks and devilish laughter in the middle of a Brazilian night made our blood run cold. And there were the stories our friend, Vera, told us. They made the spiritual battle very personal. The spiritual struggle was real indeed!

Yet I talked to missionaries who denied that there was any demonic activity in Brazil "in these days." I was stunned. I was even more confused when a Brazilian pastor dismissed the subject, commenting about exaggerated stories and spiritual immaturity. Other missionaries with whom I talked accepted the reality of evil powers. But they were so afraid of the demons that, like the Israelite army, they were on the sidelines, avoiding any engagement with the enemy. They lived in a kind of pretend world, going about their missionary activity and ignoring the possibility of any demonic opposition to it.

It Was Time for Some Self-Analysis

Standing before this "Goliath" of spiritism, I had to analyze *my* position. For me, would it be fear or faith? What would be my standing in the ranks? Would it be spiritual readiness, or a futile trust in my learning and "equipment"? I was tempted to think, *If I had just one more seminar— If I had read that book a little more carefully— But, I haven't had that course—* Thoughts like that were more than a temptation. I *thought* them! Like David trying to wear Saul's oversized armor, I was beginning to trust in my equipment and not in my God.

The army of Israel was passively maintaining a state of avoidance. The whole function of an army is to fight, and to fight as a unit, as one body. In so doing, each member can help defend his fellow soldiers. There is a certain strength in numbers.

The raw truth is we are in the battle against these forces of darkness already. Whether or not we want to be there, we *are* there. Paul says "Our struggle is . . . against the rulers, against the authorities, against the powers of this dark world and against the spiritual forces of evil in the heavenly realms" (Ephesians 6:12). That sounds suspiciously like demonic powers under Satan's control. *We are in the battle.* The only remaining question is, Are we ready for this spiritual battle? Or are we, like the army of Israel, passively trying to avoid the action?

I was teaching a class of Brazilian Christians on the reality of spiritual warfare. There were 14 people in the class. I asked how many had been involved in spiritist activities before turning to Christ. All 14 raised their hands.

Not Only in Brazil

Once I was driving in Brazil with a friend, and we came to a spiritist's offering spread out in the road. The offering was more than a yard wide. The centerpiece was a freshly severed goat's head. There was beer and bread. There were apples, cigars, peanuts and a variety of other things.

"There really *are* people who worship the spirits, aren't there?" commented my friend. Yes. And not just in Brazil. The influx of Eastern religions, drugs and a host of other evils has inundated North America with demonic activity. Once we enjoyed a certain immunity from these evil forces. But no longer.

If we are truly *in* this battle, we meed to identify our enemy. A rapid reconnaissance of the Scriptures reveals him in detail. Just by noting his names and titles, we get a fairly accurate assessment of him and his operation. He is the deceiver. An angel of light. A liar and the father of lies. He is the chief accuser of the saints. A murderer. A thief. And for every believer, he is the adversary.

Unfortunately, many unprepared "soldiers" get distracted by curiosity and a misdirected attention to some of the events of the battle. They want to hear more stories, more details—not of victory over the enemy but of the enemy's manifestations. Often they end up with a headful of information from the evil spirit manifesting itself through someone. They forget that the spirit, too, is a liar and a deceiver.

As Paul says, we need to "be strong in the Lord and in his mighty power." We must "put on the full armor of God so that [we] can take [our] stand against the devil's schemes" (Ephesians 6:10-11). We need to look to our victorious Lord. We need to focus on the authority and victory that is ours in Christ Jesus.

"Evangelical Spiritism"

Once I was praying with a Christian woman in Porto Alegre. She had a physical need and was also involved in a spiritual struggle. She herself was praying when suddenly she stopped. I looked up to see if anything was wrong. She took a silver ring from her finger and handed it to me.

"Pastor, do you know what this is?" she asked me. She proceeded to explain that she had bought the ring and wore it because it was supposed to bring good health. "It's not right, is it, for me to pray and trust God if I'm trusting the power of this ring?"

The woman recognized her compromise, her involvement in what could be called spiritual adultery—trusting Jesus, but also trusting demonic powers.

Daily in Brazil I see literally thousands of Christian stickers—Bible verses and Christian slogans. They are pasted on cars in São Paulo. There are so many you could almost have devotions reading them in a traffic jam! At first I thought, *What boldness these Christians have!* Then I noticed that some of these same cars bore little ribbons, used in a superstitious way to protect the car or its occupants. I discovered that even evangelical Christians use these things to protect their cars from being stolen!

Does this "evangelical spiritism"—a syncretism of spirit appeasement and Christian faith—happen just in Brazil? Ask your Christian friends if they read the horoscopes in the newspaper. Ask them why they put salt in the corners of their houses. Or carry a rabbit's foot. Or have a plastic bag of water hanging in the window. Could there be evangelical spiritism in North America, too?

Are we truly *in* the battle? Or are we siding with the enemy? Have we, knowingly or otherwise, borrowed the enemy's pagan ways and incorporated them into our Christian lives?

What the Word of God Says

An old saint wisely advises us that *we must build our beliefs and practices about spiritual warfare on God's Word.* Personal experience and demonic revelations won't do. God has listed for us in Ephesians 6:14-17 the items of our spiritual armor:

The belt of truth

The breastplate of righteousness
On our feet the readiness that comes from
the gospel of peace
The shield of faith
The helmet of salvation
The sword of the Spirit, which is the Word
of God

With it all, we are to "pray in the Spirit on all occasions with all kinds of prayers and requests" (6:18).

Are we prepared for battle? We analyze and double-check the pieces of our armor and its readiness. We emphasize and reemphasize our position alongside our colleagues, our fellow believers. We are convinced that our Lord is strong and mighty. He is sufficient to overcome the enemy's fear tactics and our own personal misgivings. In Christ we come to understand the enemy-victor relationship and where we stand among the ranks of the faithful.

The helmet of salvation and the shield of faith are reminders of our conversion and Christian life. Yes, the gospel has made a genuine difference in my life. No, I am not *just* convinced of this; I am converted! I am a new creation in Jesus Christ! In my daily process of self-examination, the statements of Jesus about vine and branches and fruit (John 15) are no longer cliches. The Gardener sees that I am truly attached to the Vine. He prunes me so that I might be more fruitful.

The Word of God plays an important part in my preparation for battle. It helps to link me to God and His will. It is a mirror by which I examine my readiness to live for God and my loyalty to Him. Without this armor of God, I am not equipped to combat the satanic powers against which I am pitted.

Sanctification Is Essential

Knowing the enemy's strength and design motivates me to sanctified living. Concisely stated, I am to be pure, godly and God-equipped for spiritual conflict. I am to have in place my breastplate of righteousness. A friend once tried to tell me that the state of a person's spiritual life really doesn't matter in the exercise of our spiritual gifts and in spiritual warfare. I disagree completely! Granted the authority and power of Christ are untarnishable. But Christ demands clean hands and a pure heart (Psalm 24:3-4). He commands me to be holy (Romans 12:1).

I recall a long conversation I once had with a missionary in the Philippines. He related how an evil spirit had manifested itself in one of the church members. Missionaries and pastors gathered in her home to exorcise the spirit. But the spirit began denouncing the "soldiers" one by one, citing immorality and sin in their personal lives. Most of those who had gone there to pray left the house in embarrassment and fear. The woman remained demonized.

Does our own spiritual state play a. part in our readiness for battle? Most definitely! That is why Peter warns us that Satan "prowls around like a roaring lion looking for someone to devour" (1 Peter 5:8). He advises us to "resist him, standing firm in the faith" (5:9), to "be self-controlled and alert" (5:8).

I ask again: Are we ready for battle? Have we

identified the enemy? Are we in a victorious relationship with Christ our Lord? Have we truly been transformed by Him? Are we daily living in personal holiness? Are we progressively being conformed to Christ's image and purpose? If the answer is yes, we are ready for battle!

The Defensive Aspect

Notice also in Ephesians 6 the defensive aspect of spiritual warfare. Paul underscores this with words such as "be strong," "stand firm," "resist," "avoid." In his book, *Ephesians: Power and Magic,* Clinton E. Arnold addresses this perspective. He reminds us that the authority the believer has in Christ "is power for a purpose—to resist the evil angelic 'powers.' It is power for ethical Christian conduct and mission." Ephesians 6:13 also implies this defensive posture: "Put on the full armor of God, so that *when* the day of evil comes, you may be able to stand your ground" (emphasis added). This defensive aspect speaks to the need for inward growth, Christian development and the building up of the church as a whole.

Why Are We in This Battle?

The army of Israel preferred not to fight. For the Christian, that is hardly an option. Either we fight or we are "devoured" by the "roaring lion." Nevertheless, we do well to examine our motives as we enter this battle with the powers of darkness and evil.

Sometimes we are called to make a frontal assault on the demonic powers. Some enter the battle aggressively. They relish the self-glory. They want to be known for their boldness. But the seven sons of

Sceva (Acts 19:13-17) testify to the folly of such a stance. This attitude tends also to be egocentric. We deny or overlook our colleagues who are fighting the battle alongside us.

Some enter the battle out of curiosity. They want to see what is going to happen. I sensed this strongly once. I reasoned, *Wouldn't it be interesting to use this opportunity as an experiment? God's power is so great, and the enemy's tactics are so very intriguing.* But the concepts of unity and camaraderie enter the picture here, too. We must respect the dignity of the person whom the evil spirits may be manipulating. We must not let the demonic activity distract us from the goals of deliverance and victory. We enter the battle in order to see lives restored in Jesus Christ. We enter the battle to see men and women liberated to serve the Master freely and joyfully.

Sometimes we are going to be disappointed. Several years ago I had my first in-depth involvment in a case of demonization. The man was so dramatically delivered from the spirits that had bound him that I wrote up his story for our denominational magazine.

Many people who read my article have later asked me, "Has the man remained firm in Christ? Is he still 'attached to the Vine'"? Sadly, I must answer no. The man has not remained attached to the Vine. This outcome is an unpleasant reminder that the battle is about lives. It is about the perseverance of the saints in their service for Christ. This is warfare. Warfare is never easy. It demands the utmost from us.

The Battle Is Real

The battle is on! It is real! We identify the enemy

so we may confront him for who he is and as he is. We do so confidently because of our victorious relationship in Jesus Christ. In Him we have authority and power. In Him we have salvation and freedom. In Him we have holiness to live pure lives dedicated to doing His will.

Putting on the whole armor of God is a defensive act as we prepare for battle. At the same time it is a missionary act. Are we not to have on our feet "the readiness that comes from the gospel of peace"? Our mission is to see that people are freed from satanic bondage (Isaiah 61:1). By the power that God supplies, we are to release them to live joyously, victoriously in Christ Jesus.

It is time to step from the sidelines. It is time to enter the battlefield with courage and confidence. God has called us. Multitudes yet need to enter His kingdom. Will you join me?

CHAPTER 22

Missions and the Mobilized Church

by Clarence D. Croscutt

THE CHURCH IN ACTS IS THE STORY of a church on the move. The picture Luke draws in the early part of his book is a picture of people mobilized by the Spirit of God. Disciples who had been "looking into the sky" (Acts 1:11) as Jesus ascended were launched into action as the Spirit descended. Luke summarizes the results of the first day's action in these words:

> *Those who accepted [Peter's] message were baptized, and about three thousand were added to their number that day.*
> *They devoted themselves to the apostles' teaching and to the fellowship, to the breaking of bread and to prayer. Everyone was filled with awe, and many wonders and miraculous signs were done by the apostles. All the believers were together and had everything in common. Selling their possessions and goods, they gave to anyone as he had need. Every day they continued to meet together in the temple courts. They broke bread in their homes and ate together with glad and sincere*

hearts, praising God and enjoying the favor of all the people. And the Lord added to their number daily those who were being saved. (Acts 2:41-47)

The original company, "numbering about a hundred and twenty" (Acts 1:15), obediently and prayerfully waited in that "upstairs" room in Jerusalem. At God's appointed time He empowered them with His Spirit, and they marched out like a mobilized army to begin their witness for Jesus.

I ask: *Does God really want anything less from the church of Jesus Christ today?*

Mobilization Is a War Word

Repeat: The Acts record carries with it the sense of a church on the move. It was mobilized by the Divine Presence. *Mobilized* is an appropriate term to describe what was happening to the young church. It's a word created in the context of war. It means "to put into movement or circulation," "to assemble and make ready for war duty," "to marshal (as resources) for action." The early church was a church on the move.

In my state of Pennsylvania, the winter of 1996 will be remembered for its heavy snows and disastrous floods. For just such emergencies, the Federal Emergency Management Agency (FEMA) has a roster of experts across the country. These men and women are on call. When the floods hit Pennsylvania (and later Oregon), FEMA mobilized these disaster experts to assist the flood victims.

In a similar sense, the United States Air Force has formed the Strategic Air Command. It is poised to scramble at once to avert any breach of America's air defenses. That same sense of preparedness marked the early church. But its members were *opportunity* experts. The church was poised and ready for every opportunity to witness for Christ. Such readiness should mark the church of Jesus Christ yet today.

Israel Was a Nation on the Move

The Old Testament portrays an interactive God— One who is always influencing His people no matter where their location. He found Abraham in Ur of the Chaldees (present-day Iraq). He followed Abraham to Haran (present-day Turkey). There He called him to journey still farther west and south to the land of promise.

Two generations later, God took the Israelites into Egypt—and in course of time delivered them from Egypt. For 40 years in the desert, the tent pegs of the tabernacle were never driven too deeply into the sand, for Israel was a nation on the move.

Even after Israel had settled in Canaan, the nation forfeited its tranquility through gross disobedience. Ten of the tribes were deported into Assyria. The remnants of the two southern tribes ended up in Babylonia. Wherever they were driven and wherever they migrated, the people of Israel became a witness to the one true God. Daniel and his three friends were influential in the highest echelons of the Babylonian Empire. Who can forget Nehemiah, cupbearer to the Persian king Artaxerxes, or Queen Esther, consort to the fabled Xerxes? By the time of the Grecian Empire, Jews had settled in Alexandria and other major cities. The Greek translation of the Old Testament Scriptures (the Septuagint) brought to Grecian pagans a knowledge of the Lord God.

Passion: The Wings on Which the Church Moves

If mobilization marked the activity of the early church, passion marked its spirit. The church had a passion for people. It is obvious in the text quoted earlier:

> Those who accepted [Peter's] message were baptized, and about three thousand were added to their number that day.
> They devoted themselves to the apostles' teaching and to the fellowship, to the breaking of bread and to prayer. . . . All the believers were together and had everything in common. Selling their possessions and goods, they gave to anyone as he had need. (Acts 2:41-42, 44-45)

The passion of the early church is evident in the Christians' concern for each other. The members willingly gave possessions, time and food for the comfort of the whole body. It is also evident in the apostles' devotion to Jesus. Flogged unjustly by the Jewish Sanhedrin (Acts 5:40-41) they walked away "rejoicing because they had been counted worthy of suffering disgrace for the Name."

A fellow worker and I were discussing the "good old days" as we lingered at the table after Sunday dinner. Of course, neither of us was actually present in that era, but we had read extensively about it.

"That's the missing dimension in our churches today," my friend commented. "The early days were saturated with a passion for Jesus Himself above all other desires."

Missions and evangelism fail not for lack of money—though money seems never quite enough. They fail not for resources of personnel and tools, though both are in short supply. Official red tape and the denial of visas are not the major obstacles. Missions and evangelism fail because we are not borne up by the wings of passion for the Savior and the people He died for. It was passion for Jesus that motivated the apostles. They had heard His command when He ascended; they had been stirred to action by the wind of His Spirit. Peter's message on the day of Pentecost breathed that passion into the attentive onlookers. Jesus, and Jesus only, was their watchword.

We need to feel this passion in our church missionary conferences. World evangelization is dear to God's heart (John 3:16); it should be dear to ours. If we truly love Jesus, we will

- prepare the church building tastefully in celebration of missions
- clear our own schedules so that we can be present at every public service of the conference
- see that our families, particularly our children, are prepared for what will take place
- be interested in hearing what He has to say to us through the missionaries and other speakers
- pray for a miraculous provision of funds for our church's missionary enterprise

This passion for a lost world, borne by a love for Jesus and His heart's desire, can easily be dampened. Frequently it is suppressed by the most insignificant things: busy schedules, demanding requests, our own selfish, personal interests. I know from regretful experience. This passion, however, can give lift to a heart tending to be tethered to this earth, snagged by the relatively trivial.

Terry Teykl, executive director of Renewal Ministries, quotes a comment made by John Newton, the derelict seaman who found Christ: "A soul disengaged from the world is a heavenly one; and then we are ready for heaven when our heart is there before us."

Prayer: The Fuel of Godly Passion

A passion for the Savior and for lost people is not all that our text speaks of. Luke, the writer of Acts, reports:

> They devoted themselves to . . . prayer.
> (Acts 2:42)

We can praise God for a rekindled interest within the church in prayer! If passion is dormant, we can revive it only as we seek God's face in prayer. This kind of passion cannot be manipulated or managed, as our corporations try to do. Prayer alone fuels passion.

I am learning that prayer is not really for God's benefit. We do not pray in order to inform Him of what is happening in our world. It is not like the gentleman's prayer I heard about. He began with the words, "O Lord, as Thou knowest from this morning's newspaper—" Neither do we pray in order to bribe God to act in the manner we think He should. Prayer is for the purpose of listening to the only true God who still speaks to His people. Ezekiel's words continue to be relevant:

> Then the nations around you that remain will know that I the LORD have rebuilt what was destroyed and have replanted what was desolate. I the LORD have spoken, and I will do it.
> This is what the Sovereign LORD says: Once again I will yield to the plea of the house of Israel and do this for them: I will make their people as numerous as sheep. (Ezekiel 36:36-37)

Here is something we can be assured that God will do—once again. He says, "I will yield to the plea of the house of Israel and do this for them." Can a person be devoted to Jesus and have no real interest in praying about his or her involvement in world witness? The answer is apparent.

The mobilized church is fueled, moreover, by *individual* prayer. This kind of praying is the "closet" type that Jesus spoke of. He said: "Again, I tell you that if two of you on earth agree about anything you ask for, it will be done for you by my Father in heaven. For where two or three come together in my name, there am I with them" (Matthew 18:19-20).

Terry Teykl, whom I referred to earlier, reports:

> God is doing a new thing in prayer today; His call is going forth! The interest in personal prayer and spiritual formation is on the rise. Every day 170 million Christians pray for the Great Commission. There are 10 million prayer groups meeting across [America] and 1,400 prayer networks coordinating prayer from city to city. Local chur-

ches are praying in new and exciting ways. Even whole denominations are mobilizing to pray, and the Denominational Prayer Leaders Network meets to coordinate major prayer efforts. In Cleveland, Tennessee, the Church of God has a ministry called "Prayerborne" that is made up of 5,000 retirees who are praying for spiritual awakening in their church and city. The Southern Baptist Church has set goals to place prayer coordinators in states, associations and local churches.

In the church that I pastor, prayer is one of the most important ingredients in our annual missionary conference. We witness a full church at every evening service throughout the week. As a church, we are convinced that faithful prayer results in a generous missionary faith promise offering as well. We pray individually, we pray in home-based small group gatherings, we pray in concerts of prayer lasting into the small hours of the morning. And God answers from resolving weather problems to keeping staff healthy to building a momentum of excitement for the missionary enterprise.

Terry Teykl quotes Samuel Chadwick: "The one concern of the devil is to keep Christians from praying. He fears nothing from prayerless studies, prayerless work and prayerless religion. He laughs at our toil, mocks at our wisdom, but trembles when we pray."

My wife received word from a relative in her home church that an older, dearly loved saint had gone to be with the Lord. Her last words as she left this life were whispered prayers for missionaries. Imagine the reward awaiting her for a life fueled by such commitment to prayer!

Progress: Running without Weariness

On the tropical island of Aneityum in the South Pacific lies the grave of John Geddie, pioneer Canadian Presbyterian missionary. On the stone marker is this epitaph: "When he landed in 1848, there were no Christians; when he left in 1872, there were no heathens." Geddie, under God's empowering, made a difference. Are you making a spiritual difference where you are?

A mobilized church is a church on the move. "Only the moving ship can be steered," runs an old adage. In the spiritual dimension, believers cannot be mobilized unless they are in spiritual motion. Believers who are not a part of world evangelization lose that vital spiritual speed and become self-centered, careless and bored.

Earlier I observed the mobility of the Israelites. From the patriarchs onward, each geographical transition brought the knowledge of the Lord God to a new group of people.

So it was with the early church. Philip was directed by God to go to the desert road running from Jerusalem to Gaza. He obeyed and led the treasurer of Ethiopia to saving faith (Acts 8:26-38). Paul and Silas, actively pursuing missionary work in Asia Minor, saw the vision of a Macedonian man begging them to come his way. The churches in Philippi, Thessalonica, Corinth and other European cities resulted.

God still wants that to happen. Make sure you don't drive your tent pegs too firmly into the ground where you are. Don't get too attached to your present locale. God may have another place in mind. Willingness to be mobile just may be the reason why the church in China is advancing so phenomenally. In his stirring book, *The Church in China*, Carl Lawrence quotes a Chinese believer who says in part:

> These [Chinese] saints who have gone down into the furnace, far from being harmed, have had their faces glorified and their spirits filled with power, with greater authority to preach the Word and a far more abundant life. . . .
>
> God has placed us in these last days to wage war so that the number of those saved will increase through us, and that His will shall be fulfilled through us in this generation. He desires us to advance into glory with Him. So making the most of the very short time left, let us continually do the work of the Lord. . . . There are still . . . many lambs wandering in the mountains and high peaks without any to seek and find them. May the Lord Jesus place a burden to preach the gospel on each laborer's heart and give a spirit of prayer to each Christian [to] become a prayer warrior.

Lawrence concludes with these words of his own:

> From my padded pew, in my air-conditioned sanctuary, holding my computerized mailing list, an ad for a new version of the Bible, subscription reminders for three Christian magazines and several invitations to "giant spiritual rallies," I withhold comment—not because of a lack of words, but an inability to speak.

Soon We Will Be Home

A mobilized church is motivated by more than a desire to be big. That is tantamount to driving a car for the simple reason that you have a license. We ought to be on the move, not for growth's sake, but because we have a place to which we are going. We have a purpose for living and a passion for Jesus fueled by "listening" prayer.

The Scriptures comment that Abraham, when called to Canaan, lived there "in tents. . . . For he was looking forward to the city with foundations, whose architect and builder is God" (Hebrews 11:9-10). No matter how challenging the place where God sends you as His witness, it is only a layover on the journey to heaven!

Soon—perhaps very soon—this mobilized church will assume the dimensions of a victorious army returning home. From the layovers in Chile and China, Guinea and Gabon and our own neighborhoods, workplaces and homes, we will come. We will be on the move for the final time. We will be on our way home! And with us will be those from every tribe and language and people and nation who have put their trust in our Savior.

The task of the mobilized church is one taught by prayer and armed with passion: to take home with her as many people as possible.

Missions and the Unreached People Groups

by Fred H. Smith

D AVID HUNTER WAS FACED WITH A dilemma for which Bible college had not prepared him. At the time, he was a relatively new missionary to a tribe of people who had not before heard the good news of salvation. Part of his message to his adopted people had been the promise of eternal life. And now one of his first converts was dead.

The non-Christians claimed the spirits had taken her in punishment for leaving the gods of her fathers. The few other believers—all of them new in the faith—were wavering. What was he to tell them?

Since the deceased woman was a Christian, representatives from her village wanted David to perform whatever ceremony for the dead that Christians perform. He agreed, but as he canoed down the river to the village he pondered his dilemma. How could he preach about eternal life over a dead body? He arrived at the village still uncertain about what to say. He made his way through the restless crowd of villagers. Praying one last time for wisdom, he stepped into the hut where the dead woman lay.

As David faced the expectant group of people circled around their departed relative, God brought to his mind some Scripture. He quoted these words:

> After this I looked and there before me was a great multitude that no one could count, from every nation, tribe, people and language, standing before the throne and in front of the Lamb. They were wearing white robes and were holding palm branches in their hands. And they cried out in a loud voice:
>
> "Salvation belongs to our God,
> who sits on the throne,
> and to the Lamb." (Revelation 7:9-10)

Triumphantly David turned to the people. "Today," he declared, "this tribe has its first representative before the throne of God. Up to this time you had no one there, but now you do!" David paused to let this announcement sink in. In the silence the villagers began to assimilate what he had said. And then, as if on cue, everyone burst into joy and dancing. *For the first time in their history they were represented before the throne of God!*

Many Others Are Still Isolated

That Scripture and David Hunter's story highlight God's concern that those from "every tribe, and language and people and nation" (Revelation 5:9) be present in heaven. The story also aptly illustrates our need to become involved in taking the gospel to the unreached people groups of the world. One person in five is in this category—a total numbering more than 1.1 *billion* people. It is not simply that they have refused to receive Christ's offer of salvation. It is not even that they have never heard the good news. Rather, *in their situation it is unlikely they will have opportunity to hear the good news unless someone from the outside goes to them.* Thus the name, Unreached People Groups (UPG).

Unreached people groups exist on all seven continents, in every country and at all socio-economic levels. These groups, some extensive, some very small, live in isolation from any probable Christian witness. Unless a cross-cultural servant of God's kingdom, *a missionary,* goes to them, they likely *never* will have an opportunity to know who Jesus is and what He has done for them.

The unreached could be isolated Somalians wandering in the East Africa desert.They could be Uzbek tribesmen deep in the heart of Asia. The unreached could be young members of a Los Angeles street gang in an environment that has deprived them of hope.

The unreached could be the kin of the old wrinkled miner I encountered in the isolated regions of the Peruvian Andes. I had been taken to his little adobe hut by a mutual friend. I was to talk to him about Jesus. Once my eyes adjusted to the interior darkness, I saw the only piece of furniture in the hut. It was an open casket standing against one wall. The man knew he had little remaining time. Black lung disease was taking its toll. So he had spent his last *soles* to prepare for certain death. His only possessions were the clothes he wore, a faded poncho in which he wrapped himself at night—and his casket. I shared the gospel with that dying man. As I spoke, the Holy Spirit penetrated his darkened heart and he accepted Jesus as his Savior!

They Could Be the Wealthy

The unreached could as easily be the pampered super-rich: Japanese millionaires, isolated by Shintoism and wealth, surveying their business empires. They could be Cali drug lords or Middle East oil sheiks.

We are talking about the *unreached,* not just the unevangelized. There is a philosophy that promotes every unsaved person as unreached. That simply is not the case! An unsaved person *may* be an unreached person, but not necessarily.

An unreached person has little likelihood of hearing the gospel unless an *outsider* takes the message to him or her. The gospel and the church may be present within the geographical boundaries of his or her country. But status, employment, language or other barriers prevent him or her from hearing it. He or she is unsaved *and* unreached.

On the other hand, an unsaved person may nevertheless have been reached by the gospel. He or she has heard the message of salvation but for whatever reason has refused to accept it. While not *unreached,* he or she remains *unsaved* and outside the kingdom of God. He or she is as spiritually lost and destitute as any unreached person. The difference has to do with *opportunity* to accept the message. The unreached exist in isolation that precludes the probability of their hearing the good news of Jesus.

Unreached people, whether pygmies of central Africa or the elite of Paris, will not likely hear the good news of salvation unless outside missionaries penetrate their isolation. But why are missionaries necessary to reach the unreached? Why does someone other than a Sasak of Indonesia have to go to the Sasaks with the gospel? The answer is simple but sad. *There are no Christians among the 1,850,000 Sasaks.* There are no believers to share with their fellow Sasaks the message of salvation. Unless someone from the outside enters their ranks, they will not have the chance to believe in Jesus Christ.

Many Unreached Groups Are in Our Cities

As I have suggested, these unreached people are found not only on the fringes of rural society. They can also be found within urban populations. The Javanese community of Suriname is an example. Suriname is a small country in northern South America, about as far from the Indonesian island of Java as it is can be. In 1996 the Alliance Chinese Church of Paramaribo, Suriname, plans to initiate a gospel ministry among this unreached group of Muslims. A Javanese Christian and his Dutch wife will be supported by the Chinese Christian community to present the 62,000 Javanese of Suriname with the claims of the gospel.

The unreached can be found in the upper levels of society. In Lima, there is a church committed to reaching the upper-middle- and upper-class Peruvians. These men and women have material goods and wealth, but they know not how to attain eternal life. Why? Because their religion has not told them! And all their friends are likewise without that knowledge.

If a religion does not answer life's most important

questions, or misrepresents God's Word, then the hearers of that misrepresentation are as lost and unreached as the most ignorant of savages.

That raises another issue. What if people have heard a distorted gospel? Have they "heard"? In some cases, possibly yes. But is what they heard the truth? Unless the knowledge they receive leads them to decide for or against Jesus Christ the Savior, they remain as ignorant as one who has never heard.

I am burdened for those more than 1.1 billion who have never seen a Bible. People who have never heard even once of Jesus Christ. People who never will hear unless someone goes to them. The missionaries who go to them will have the priceless joy of freeing some of Satan's captives. They will see changed lives. As the chains of bondage snap, there will be laughter for sorrow, smiles instead of tears, light rather than darkness.

As this book so adequately argues, the task of missions is still incomplete. As long as one people group is unrepresented before God's throne, we have an ongoing responsibility. People need to hear the life-changing message of a Savior and Lord who died and rose again. Especially those who have no other means of hearing it.

Why So Long?

After almost 2,000 years, there are still thousands of unreached people groups. One in five lives in an isolation that prohibits him or her from hearing of God's love in Christ Jesus. Why? A major reason is that Satan has had these millenniums to build effective barriers around them. God's people need to agree together to pray down those barriers. God's people need to pray forth harvesters and thus speed the King's return.

> *And this gospel of the kingdom will be preached in the whole world as a testimony to all nations, and then the end will come.* (Matthew 24:14)

There is a second reason why the job is not yet finished. The difficulty of reaching some of these groups has isolated them from the gospel. Conflicting ideologies, other religions and politics have produced, in some instances, nearly insurmountable barriers. Sometimes, too, the church is at fault. Misplaced priorities and poor stewardship of resources can blunt the church's response. So can an outmoded understanding of the missionary task.

No single church denomination or missionary agency can reach all the unreached people groups. But in cooperative effort with like-minded Christians we can complete the task. We can bring the unreached into the fold of the reached *and* saved.

An "Exhibit A" Example

In the Indonesian province of Irian Jaya, missionaries have now worked for more than 40 years. The transformation among once warring tribes in the island's interior has been radical.

An Indonesian official had heard about these very positive changes within one tribe and wanted to confirm for himself their reality. Flying to Sentani, near the coast, he boarded a smaller plane, in company with a missionary, for the trip to the interior. Their destination: Mapnduma, in the fabled Baliem Valley. Arriving at Mapnduma, the official was amazed by what he saw. He sincerely congratulated the assembled villagers on the positive changes in their lifestyle. An old man stood up, wanting to respond. At first the missionary, who was interpreting, was reluctant to let him speak. He feared the elderly man might embarrass the villagers. But the man politely insisted until the missionary relented.

Going to the podium, the man held up a small vial on its edge and tapped it, obviously expecting something to come out. Nothing happened. He tapped the vial again. Still no action. Finally he reached in with his fingers and pulled out a live cockroach. He held up the cockroach for all to see.

"Before the missionary came," the old man began, "we were like this cockroach, living in a dark pit. Even as the cockroach is comfortable living in such surroundings, so were we. We knew nothing better." He threw the cockroach to the ground, where it promptly scurried off to seek a hiding place.

Turning to the official, the man continued: "But the missionary showed us how to get out of the pit and into the light. And ever since, our lives have been changed!"

We Are to Be Involved

So it was with us. Someone told *us* how to get out of sin's dark pit we were living in. Now we are to be involved in taking the gospel to every nation and tribe and people and language. Especially urgent is our obligation to the more than 1.1 billion unreached people. They have yet to receive an understandable presentation of the good news. We need to pray that God will send forth laborers to scale the barriers that keep them in darkness and sin.

We need to "enflesh" the gospel among them. They have a need and a right to see what being a follower of Christ is all about. We individuals, and the churches we are members of, need to be involved in the task of bringing back the King. He will not return until this gospel of the kingdom is "preached in the whole world as a testimony to all nations."

You and I play important roles in the King's return. Let's finish the job!

Participating Authors

Note: All of the authors are related to
The Christian and Missionary Alliance.

Dr. Norman E. Allison, former missionary to Jordan, is Director, School of World Missions, Toccoa Falls (Georgia) College and professor of anthropology at the college.

Dr. Keith M. Bailey, pastor, church administrator, conference speaker, lives in retirement in Dayton, Ohio.

Dr. Paul F. Bubna is President of Alliance Theological Seminary, Nyack, New York.

Dr. Arnold L. Cook, former missionary to Latin America, is President, The Christian and Missionary Alliance in Canada.

Miss Joy E. Corby, after two missionary terms in Gabon, Africa, currently works with Wheaton (Illinois) Youth Outreach.

Rev. H. Robert Cowles, missionary to the Philippines, editor of *Alliance Life* and executive vice-president of Christian Publications, lives in retirement in Carlisle, Pennsylvania.

Rev. Clarence D. Croscutt is Senior Pastor, C&MA Church, DuBois, Pennsylvania.

Rev. Rockwell L. Dillaman is Senior Pastor, Allegheny Center Alliance Church, Pittsburgh, Pennsylvania.

Mr. J. Evan Evans, together with his wife, Jewel, are dorm parents at International Christian Academy, Bouaké, Côte d'Ivoire, West Africa.

Dr. K. Neill Foster, whose preaching ministry has taken him worldwide, is Executive Vice-President/Publisher, Christian Publications, Camp Hill, Pennsylvania.

Dr. Wendell K. Grout for many years was Senior Pastor, First Alliance Church, Calgary, Alberta. Now retired, he lives in Priddis, Alberta.

Rev. Fred A. Hartley, III, a popular author, is Senior Pastor, Lilburn (Georgia) Alliance Church.

Rev. Steve M. Irvin, a missionary in Colombia, is involved in international evangelism.

Rev. David P. Jones, after more than 25 years of missionary service in Brazil, is Director for Missions Mobilization.

Dr. Louis L. King, former missionary administrator, is a past president of The Christian and Missionary Alliance.

Mrs. Jean A. Livingston, with her husband, Jim, has served as a missionary in Vietnam and more recently in the Philippines.

Rev. David O. Manske, together with his wife, Susanna, are missionaries to Brazil. They also served as missionaries-in-residence at Crown College, St. Bonifacius, Minnesota.

Rev. Peter N. Nanfelt is Vice-President, Division of Overseas Ministries.

Dr. Fred H. Smith is Regional Director for Latin America North.

David C. Thompson, M.D., is Director, Bongolo Evangelical Hospital, Lebamba, Gabon.

Rev. Harvey A. Town, former missionary to Japan, is Superintendent, Rocky Mountain District.

Dr. A.W. Tozer, pastor, writer and conference speaker, was editor of *Alliance Life* until his death in 1963.

Dr. Donald O. Young, former missionary to Côte d'Ivoire, West Africa, is Senior Pastor, Elberta (Alabama) Alliance Church.